Philadelphia's
LOST
WATERFRONT

Harry Kyriakodis

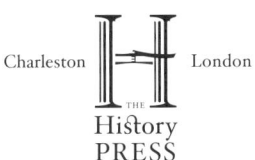

Charleston · London
The History Press

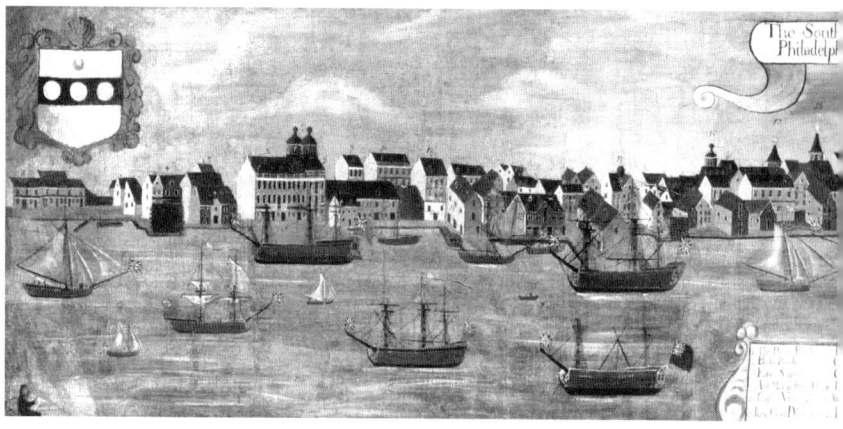

The South East Prospect of the City of Philadelphia, an oil painting by Peter Cooper from about 1720, hanging at the Library Company of Philadelphia. This work, the oldest surviving canvas of any American city, has a most interesting history. Plus, at almost eight feet long and twenty inches high, it's one of the most unusual of all paintings of Philadelphia. At either end of the canvas are the arms of

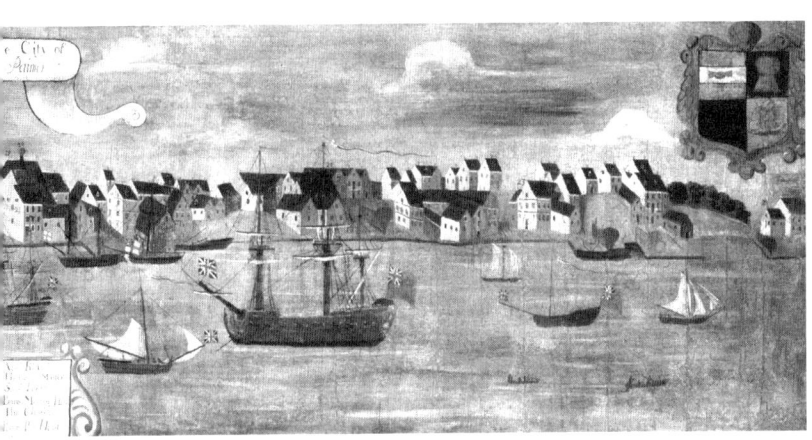

the city and the province of Pennsylvania. Beneath is a descriptive panel identifying various buildings. Despite being rather unsophisticated, the painting is practically without peer as a pictorial document of an American city. Cooper was very likely a Philadelphia sign painter. *The Library Company of Philadelphia.*

Published by The History Press
Charleston, SC 29403
www.historypress.net
Copyright © 2011 by Harry Kyriakodis
All rights reserved

Front cover, top: The Delaware River (i.e., Benjamin Franklin) Bridge under construction in 1924, looking west at the city of Philadelphia. *Delaware River Bridge Joint Commission.*

Back cover, upper black-and-white image: Delaware Avenue, looking north at the foot of Market Street, showing the Delaware Avenue El and horse-drawn wagons engaged in commercial activity along the docks, circa 1910. *Library of Congress. Lower black-and-white image*: The Chestnut Street Pier in 1901, with its rooftop recreational pavilion and pedestrian walkway over Delaware Avenue. *Philadelphia City Archives.*

First published 2011
Manufactured in the United States
ISBN 978.1.60949.371.4
Library of Congress Cataloging-in-Publication Data

Kyriakodis, Harry G.
Philadelphia's lost waterfront / Harry Kyriakodis.
p. cm.
Includes bibliographical references and index.
ISBN 978-1-60949-371-4
1. Waterfronts--Pennsylvania--Philadelphia--History. 2. Historic buildings--Pennsylvania--Philadelphia.
3. Historic sites--Pennsylvania--Philadelphia. 4. Philadelphia (Pa.)--History. 5. Delaware River Region (N.Y.-Del. and N.J.)--History. 6. Philadelphia (Pa.)--Buildings, structures, etc. 7. Philadelphia (Pa.)--Biography. 8. Philadelphia (Pa.)--Social conditions. I. Title.
F158.63.K97 2011
974.8'11--dc23
2011018584

Notice: The information in this book is true and complete to the best of our knowledge. It is offered without guarantee on the part of the author or The History Press. The author and The History Press disclaim all liability in connection with the use of this book.

All rights reserved. No part of this book may be reproduced or transmitted in any form whatsoever without prior written permission from the publisher except in the case of brief quotations embodied in critical articles and reviews.

Contents

Preface	7
Introduction	9
1. William Penn's Solution to a Touchy Dilemma in 1680s Philadelphia	13
2. At Spring Garden Street: British Barracks and Party Central on the Waterfront	19
3. Noble to Callowhill: A Romantic Stream Flowing Between a Bloody Lane and a Gallow's Hill	22
4. Callowhill to Vine: Penn's Surviving Steps and Ships and Ferries on the Frozen Delaware	28
5. The Riverfront Caves of Primitive Philadelphia	38
6. Front Street: Pennsylvania's First Street and a Kingly Highway	44
7. Vine to Race: A Calamitous Blaze and a Colossal Bridge	46
8. Race to Arch: Fighting Fires and Rats Near America's Oldest Urban Street	51
9. Arch to Market: Inventors and Millionaires by the Delaware (Enter Stephen Girard)	60

Contents

10. At Market (High) Street: Ben Franklin, King Tamanend and Christ Church in Old City Philadelphia — 74

11. Market to Chestnut: Of Ancient Taverns and Franklin's Friends on the Central Riverfront — 85

12. Chestnut to Walnut: A Welcoming Mansion (and Park) for William Penn Near the Birth of the Marines — 88

13. Walnut to Dock: Pirate Treasure, a Timeless Treaty, Troubled Taverns and a Floating Church — 95

14. Dock to South: Head House Square and a Progressive Sail Loft in Society Hill — 109

15. South of South Street: Southwark Hosts a Swedish Church and a Party for the Ages — 114

16. At Washington Avenue: Fortress to Shipyard to Navy Yard to Rail Yard to Immigration Station to Waterside Park — 120

17. Water (King) Street: A Filthy Street Triggers the Yellow Fever Epidemic of 1793 — 127

18. Delaware Avenue (Columbus Boulevard): Lost Resort Islands and Girard's Riverside Legacy — 133

19. Penn's Landing: Festivities and Tragedies on the Water — 144

20. The Delaware Expressway (I-95): Voilà—A Superhighway in the Midst — 156

Epilogue — 163
Further Reading — 165
Index — 169
About the Author — 175

Preface

Midway on Front Street, between Philadelphia's Old City and Northern Liberties neighborhoods, is a set of ancient stone steps leading down to Water Street. This narrow stairwell, on the 300 block of North Front, is a passageway to the lower street on the line of what used to be an alley called Wood Street.

The Wood Street Steps are also a passageway back in time, for they are the last of ten or so public stairways on the alley streets from Callowhill to South Streets, built about three centuries ago at the direction of William Penn, founder and proprietor of the province of Pennsylvania and founder of the city of Philadelphia. Each one of the "Penn stairs" once lay exactly on the Delaware River's western embankment, providing access to the water from the high ground of the city above. Other than Gloria Dei Church in South Philadelphia, this staircase is the only relic of the colonial era along the Delaware in Penn's City of Brotherly Love.

This account began as an investigation into these stairwells. It then broadened into a chronicle of Philadelphia's riverfront between Vine and South Streets—the city's original northern and southern boundaries. It then expanded north to Spring Garden Street and south to Washington Avenue, basically to round out the story. While the book focuses on the two-block strip of the waterfront from Front Street to the river, there are occasional forays inland to Second Street.

Preface

This study includes an exploration of the caves that Quaker settlers occupied beside the Delaware and the stories behind Front Street, Water Street and Delaware Avenue. Old City, Society Hill and Queen Village are discussed, as are the famous personalities associated with Philadelphia's riverside and the notable creeks that once crossed this zone. Shipbuilding, railroading and military activities on this stretch of the Delaware are considered, as are immigration and employment matters. Plus, extant and long-forgotten taverns, restaurants, hotels, parks, piers and places of worship are covered.

After a look at the early development of Philadelphia's original port district, the narrative proceeds block by block from Spring Garden Street to Washington Avenue. Why north to south? It just seemed better to begin with the area that still has the most remnants of the past so that some tangible evidence of Philadelphia's lost waterfront could be seen. Seeing the little that remains emphasizes how much is gone. For, ultimately, this book is a lament on all that has vanished due to the heartless routing of Interstate 95 through this two-mile-long corridor decades ago.

Contemporary happenings along the historic central waterfront of Philadelphia are highlighted in the final chapters as the narrative returns to Columbus Boulevard and Penn's Landing. It will become clear that recent conflicts concerning the use and enjoyment of the riverfront are as fresh today as they were over three hundred years ago.

I'd like to thank my family members for their support in this project, as well as my workplace colleagues and members of the Association of Philadelphia Tour Guides; also Ron Hoess, Al Johnson, Robert Kettell, Kenneth Milano, Doug Mooney, James Quilligan, Andy Sacksteder, Richard Stange, Rich Wagner and Rebecca Yamin for the informative chats and messages we exchanged. Adam Levine, a consultant for the Philadelphia Water Department, provided photos and encouragement. The staffs at the Philadelphia City Archives and the Library Company of Philadelphia were most helpful, as was The History Press team in guiding me to assemble this book.

Introduction

Great cities have great rivers, and the city of Philadelphia has two of the finest and most historic rivers in the United States: the Delaware and the Schuylkill. Both have played critical roles in the American Revolution of the eighteenth century, the Industrial and Transportation Revolutions of the nineteenth century, and even the Environmental Revolution of the twentieth century.

In the early 1680s, William Penn (1644–1718) specifically established his City of Brotherly Love at the narrowest point between these waterways to take advantage of the benefits afforded by them. In a letter to London, he gushed:

> [O]f all the many places I have seen in the world, I remember not one better seated; so that it seems to me to have been appointed for a town, whether we regard the rivers, or the conveniency of the coves, docks, springs, the loftiness and soundness of the land and the air.

Penn envisioned his colony of Pennsylvania sprawling westward from the river settlement of Philadelphia, which would serve as the colony's seat of government and base of mercantile activity.

Philadelphia's geography made it ideal as an inland seaport, and Penn's settlement responded to maritime opportunities quickly. The city became the first major shipping port in North America, so much so that a visitor in 1756 commented, "Everybody in Philadelphia deals more or less in trade."

Introduction

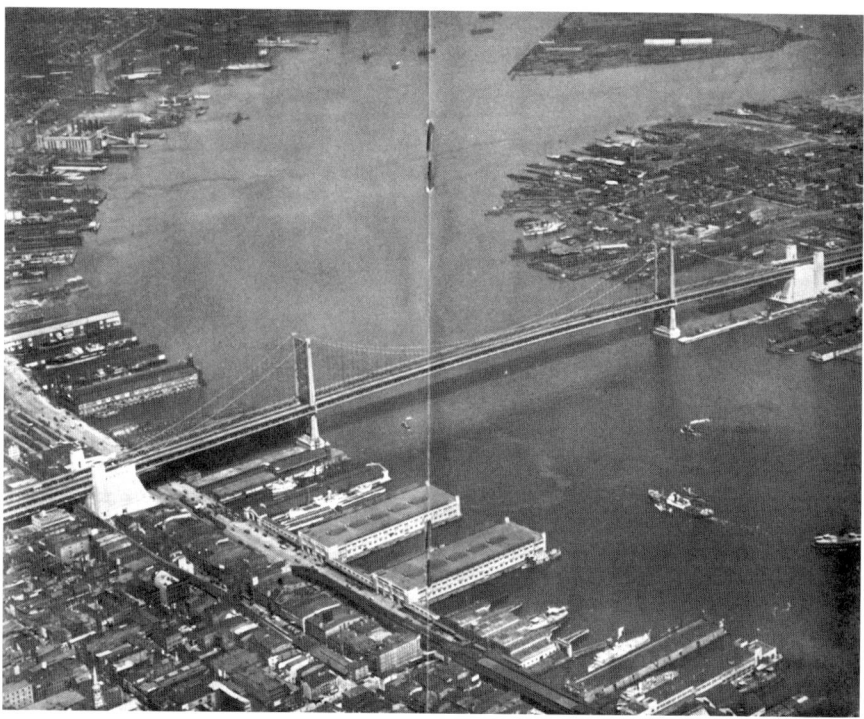

Aerial view of Philadelphia's north central waterfront, circa 1930. *Port of Philadelphia municipal publication.*

By the onset of the War for Independence, Penn's town was third only to Liverpool and London as an essential business location.

The Delaware River waterfront was the axis of the Port of Philadelphia's maritime, commercial and political bustle for some two hundred years after the city's founding. For a long time, when people outside Philadelphia thought about the city, this lively place was what came to mind—and not in a bad way.

This was where wheeling and dealing went on to encourage local, regional and national enterprise. This was where a good amount of the nation's military forces got their start. This was where transportation advances and other inventions were created and exhibited. This was where terrible urban contagions began. This was where early American capitalists made their fortunes. And this was where the individual American colonies were crafted into a nation.

Philadelphia kept its position as America's greatest trade center until the 1820s, when New York's location and financial strength bumped Penn's City to second place. Still, the city's riverfront remained the heart of town.

Introduction

But as the river district grew increasingly grim and grimy in the late nineteenth and early twentieth centuries, it started to be taken for granted and then became an afterthought. This change in regard was fostered by Philadelphia's relentless push to the west, first to the deforested area beyond Sixth Street in the 1700s, then to the City Hall neighborhood in the 1800s and then to points west, north and south in the 1900s.

As wealthy residents and merchants left the original part of Philadelphia for greener pastures, the Delaware River's edge became forlorn and unattractive—a forgotten backwater, so to speak, and certainly nothing to celebrate. The river itself practically died before World War II because of pollution, while commerce on and by the water declined dramatically afterward. The mile-wide Delaware, long the city's front door, had shut. An Interstate highway was then run through to seal the deal.

Happily, though, Philadelphia's central waterfront has been receiving attention lately. Exactly three hundred years after William Penn founded his city on the Delaware, work began on refurbishing two abandoned municipal piers at Penn's Landing for residential use. This was the first new housing along the river in over one hundred years. Other activity has followed since then, with multimillion-dollar condominiums and increased recreational, entertainment and dining venues of all sorts drawing money and movement back to this part of town. Penn's Landing has become a citywide gathering place, and even a casino has joined the mix. Philadelphia has finally rediscovered its lifeblood river and the adjoining riverfront.

All told, this is surely the most storied and interesting section of Philadelphia, as it has changed the most—for good or bad—over time. A strong case can be made that it has changed more than anyplace in America.

1
WILLIAM PENN'S SOLUTION TO A TOUCHY DILEMMA IN 1680S PHILADELPHIA

When William Penn founded Philadelphia, the area between the Delaware and Schuylkill Rivers was sparsely populated by tribes of Lenni-Lenape Native Americans (the Delaware Indians), who had inhabited villages along the Delaware for one thousand years. "Coaquannock" was their name for the region, meaning "grove of tall pines." This referred to the pine forest between the two rivers.

The Delaware Indians fished for shad by the river. These fish were so abundant in the Delaware and Schuylkill that Penn described them in correspondence: "Shads are excellent fish and of the Bigness of our Carp. They are so plentiful, that Captain Smyth's Overseer at the Skulkil, drew 600 and odd at one Draught; 300 is no wonder; 100 familiarly."

NATURAL TOPOGRAPHY

At 330 miles long, the Delaware River is the longest free-flowing river east of the Mississippi and the third longest on the East Coast. The river and bay were named after Sir Thomas West (1577–1618), the third Baron De La Warr and first governor of the colony of Virginia. The English erroneously thought that he had discovered the river, but there's no evidence that West ever saw or visited the Delaware. It was actually first explored by Henry Hudson (ca. 1570–ca. 1611), who called it "one of the finest, best, and pleasantest rivers in the world."

Philadelphia's Lost Waterfront

Along the Delaware's western bank in Philadelphia, the muddy/gravelly edge of the river originally lapped up to the future location of Water Street—a rutted lane now mostly gone in the city's old waterfront district. Immediately above this tidal flat was a sheer embankment bluff, between ten and fifty feet high, all along the local shoreline, as the river had scoured a deep channel over the eons. The top of this bluff later became Front Street, the first roadway to parallel the river when Philadelphia was planned.

Some of the city's first settlers actually lived in caves they dug into the embankment, pretty much within the space between where Front and Water Streets came to be. These shallow dugouts, long part of Philadelphia lore and described in chapter five, provided the newcomers with their initial shelter upon reaching Penn's settlement in the 1680s.

Water Street developed as the pier-head line during the eighteenth century and provided direct access to the various docks and wharves by the Delaware. As time went on, the riverfront east of Water Street became filled with "made-earth." (This is the more accurate term for landfill when hard ground is formed by piling soil and rock atop water.)

Wharves were built into the water by employing pilings and casements of logs in the shape of boxes, which were then filled with soil and stone and topped with wooden planks. As the wharves extended eastward, the planks were replaced with a harder surface, like flagstones, Belgian blocks or gravel. This eventually became solid ground, on which port structures were often erected. Docks, piers, ferry landings and the like continually moved eastward into the river in this fashion.

A series of east–west alleys cut through this new landscape over time. Commercial structures—stores, shops, lumberyards, warehouses and shipbuilding facilities—were also built on the made-earth between Water Street and the Delaware.

The embankment steps at Wood Street show how steep the western bank of the Delaware was before the march of time obliterated all traces of the riverside's original landscape.

The terrain at Vine Street had a more gradual descent to the river than that to the south—say, between Race and Market Streets—where the change in elevation was greater. Therefore, the number of actual steps (treads) composing the Wood Street stairwell is less than that of the other long-gone Penn stairways. That is to say, the other public stairs—which no longer exist—were generally more impressive than the stairwell at Wood Street. (The Wood Street Steps are covered in chapter four.)

William Penn's Solution to a Touchy Dilemma in 1680s Philadelphia

This goes to show that Philadelphia originally had two levels: 1) the main upper plane starting at Front Street and proceeding west and 2) the lower plane beside the Delaware River. This dual set of elevations can still be seen when looking at the city westward from Penn's Landing. The buildings on Front Street are much higher than those on Columbus Boulevard (formerly Delaware Avenue). Penn's Landing here is about thirty feet below the rest of Philadelphia.

In between, at its own varying elevation, is Interstate 95.

Mercantile Development

William Penn had wanted his "Greene Countrie Towne" of Philadelphia to unfold evenly between the Delaware and Schuylkill Rivers. As part of this plan, he reserved the high frontage along the Delaware for the Proprietary (or Propriety) of Pennsylvania, with land set aside for Penn and his family to use as they saw fit. This space was like the public squares that Penn

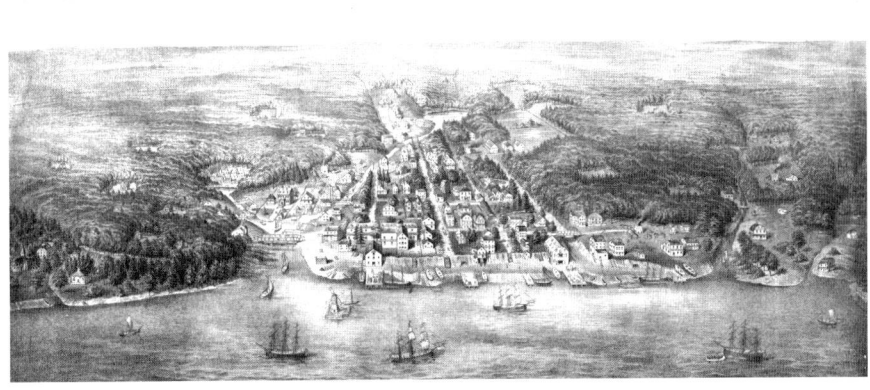

By Smith Cremens & Company, this 1875 lithograph (*Philadelphia in 1702*) sets forth a conceptual panoramic view of Philadelphia twenty years after its founding. The city occupies the space between the mouth of Dock Creek on the left and Pegg's Run on the right. Caves along the embankment and ladders to the top of the bank are visible, as are some early wharves jutting out on the Delaware. Curiously, Windmill Island is missing, although a windmill does appear just about where the long, thin isle should be. The print also contains three small views not shown here: the Penn Treaty, Philadelphia before settlement and the landing of first purchasers. *The Library Company of Philadelphia.*

designated as common parks in the four quadrants of the original city. He further hoped that a promenade with a parapet would stretch atop the length of the Delaware's west bank to provide a pleasing, uninterrupted view of the river from Front Street.

It's doubtful that Penn long pursued his plan to preserve the high ground paralleling the Delaware River for the purpose of beautifying his city. A practical man, and a shrewd real estate developer at that, he must have realized that shipping facilities had to line the edge of the river if Philadelphia was to become a prosperous commercial metropolis. This would be the only way to accommodate ships transporting merchandise and travelers to the Atlantic Coast and foreign seaports. Penn surely concluded that the riverfront would become exceedingly valuable to the Proprietary.

For all property sold in the Province of Pennsylvania, Penn used the quitrent (or ground rent) system of taxation to provide the Propriety with a steady income. Each land patent stated the annual quitrent amount for the lot. Original settlers (aka "first purchasers") were charged to pay one shilling for each one hundred acres every year. The collection of ground rents was the cause of much ill feeling between settlers and the Proprietary.

Penn and his agents sold the waterfront lots east of Front Street—the bank lots—in the 1680s. Affluent buyers, dubbed "bankers," often subdivided their lots or traded them for acreage deeper in Pennsylvania. Some had bought a thousand or more acres in the countryside and received their city lots as appurtenant to their country acquisitions, together with land in the "Liberties" (Liberty Lands) of Philadelphia County.

William Penn was soon faced with too much proposed and actual development on the Delaware riverfront. Everyone wanted to own prime real estate in the nucleus of Philadelphia, so they clustered by the river. Even more disturbing was that bankers were under the impression that they owned the waterfront abutting their holdings. The bank lot purchasers also claimed the privilege to hollow out space in the high bank next to their lots so as to create "vaults" for use as storerooms. This was the first private versus public conflict concerning the development of Philadelphia's waterfront.

Leading merchant Samuel Carpenter was the first banker to make such a demand. Early in 1684, he asked Penn for permission to "dig cellars or vaults between the Edge of the bank and [his] land provided it be done and kept without prejudice to the Road [Front Street] above." Penn rejected this request, but Carpenter returned with an even more alarming proposal. He wanted to construct a set of wharves and warehouses on his sizable bank

William Penn's Solution to a Touchy Dilemma in 1680s Philadelphia

lot between Walnut and Chestnut Streets. Such harbor structures would impede everyone's access to the river for almost a city block.

Carpenter's plan thus generated the first major controversy regarding the use of and access to Philadelphia's Delaware front. Chapter twelve has more about Samuel Carpenter, his wharf and his stairs.

WILLIAM PENN'S SOLUTION

In response to all bankers making claims on the east side of Front Street, Penn firmly declared that the riverbank was a common area owned by the Propriety—not by any banker or other first purchaser. He then softened his stance by offering a compromise. This oft-reproduced language appears in a letter dated August 3, 1684, a few days before Penn returned to England:

> *The Bank is a top common, from end to end. The rest, next* [to] *the water, belongs to front-lot men no more than* [to] *back-lot men: the way* [Front Street] *bounds them. They may build stairs—and,* [at] *the top of the bank, a common exchange, or walk; and against* [Front] *street, common wharfs may be built freely;—but into the water, and the shore, is no purchaser's.*

Thomas Jefferson called William Penn "the greatest law-giver the world has produced." Penn's declaration is an example of his Solomonic wisdom, since he devised a way to balance both public and private interests. He allowed Carpenter and other riverfront developers to build on their bank lots as they desired, but only if they allowed the public to have convenient access to the Delaware.

COOL RIVER BREEZES

Another reason for the mid-block stairways was that Penn wanted to let cool, fresh air from the Delaware River into the hot, congested city. This is echoed by Abraham Ritter in *Philadelphia and Her Merchants* (1860):

> *I may advert to a row of small two and three-story brick houses, of sombre weather-beaten hue even sixty years ago, and tell of a gap here and there between, as airholes from the river to fan the more condensed*

Philadelphia's Lost Waterfront

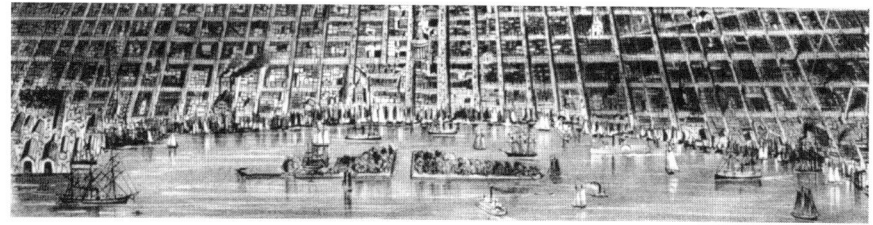

Part of a Currier-Ives print, *Bird's Eye View of Philadelphia* (1875), illustrating only the central waterfront. *Library of Congress.*

atmosphere above; or show the forethought of Father Penn in facilitating ingress and egress to and from Front to Water street by an occasional flight of stone steps.

The Penn stairs thus enabled the town and the river to stay linked both physically and ecologically.

In the end, William Penn instructed the Provincial Council of Pennsylvania to mandate that bank lot owners install stepped passageways along the Delaware River between Philadelphia's principal east–west streets. These mid-block stairs helped form strong ties between docks at the Delaware's edge (the city's "lower" level) and the core ("upper") level beginning at Front Street. Some blocks had more than one set of steps. The actual steps may have been made of wood at first and then replaced by stone as the treads rotted.

Precisely how many of these stairways were installed is unknown. The number varies from eight to twelve in the literature and gradually diminished until only the Wood Street Steps remained. Having served their original civic purpose, some stairs were closed as far back as the late eighteenth century. Others gave way to the construction of I-95 in the 1960s, but not as many as often supposed.

2

At Spring Garden Street

British Barracks and Party Central on the Waterfront

Spring Garden Street did not connect to Delaware Avenue until the 1920s, unlikely as this may seem today. The thoroughfare was first opened through the Northern Liberties District of Philadelphia County between only Sixth and Tenth Streets in the 1830s and 1840s. A landscaped portion was in the middle of the wide roadway even back then.

Military Matters (I of V): The British Barracks at Campington

A hamlet identified as Campington (later, Camptown) was once found at present-day Spring Garden Street between Second and Third. The name was attached to that locale because British troops stationed in and around Philadelphia had encamped there beginning in 1745. Barracks were built about 1753 to lodge some five thousand of the king's men. A parade ground was in the center of the garrison.

During the occupation of Philadelphia from 1777 to 1778, British soldiers stationed there manned a military post at nearby Front and Noble. Anyone exiting or entering the city to or from the north had to use that gate and present the proper military pass.

A Quaker woman named Lydia Darragh (1729–1789), on December 3, 1777, coolly walked out of town and through this gate to deliver information to General George Washington about British plans to attack his troops at Whitemarsh. It's worth learning more about this Revolutionary War spy and how her daring mission aided the American cause—but not here.

Philadelphia Warehousing and Cold Storage

The Philadelphia Warehousing and Cold Storage complex between Spring Garden and Noble Streets has been around for a long time. These bulky brick warehouses are the city's oldest and largest cold storage houses and represent the numerous long-demolished warehouses that used to line the central Philadelphia riverfront. Beach Street, an early waterside pathway analogous to Water Street, passes between the two buildings but is closed off.

Philadelphia Warehousing was incorporated in 1873 as the Mercantile Warehouse Company to enter the business of cold storage, warehousing and ice making. Its machinery included an immense boiler-house and possibly the biggest ice machine in the nation. Today, Philadelphia Cold Storage stores all manner of food, clothing and other items for anybody who wants to keep things at temperatures below twenty degrees.

The enormous American flag mural on one of the buildings is easily seen by northbound traffic on Interstate 95. A project of the Philadelphia Mural Arts Program, the six-thousand-square-foot mural was painted within two months after the terrorist attacks of September 11, 2001.

The East Central Incinerator

A low point of Philadelphia waterfront's saga was the East Central Incinerator at the foot of Spring Garden Street. This city-owned trash-burning plant was put into operation in the mid-1960s. Its construction right on the Delaware signified how disconnected the city had become from its main river by the mid-twentieth century. The massive steel and reinforced concrete structure was enclosed on two sides by the river and was supported above the water by a pier structure.

A vacant rusting eyesore for years, the incinerator was dismantled in 2002 after an environmental cleanup. Much of the site nowadays is Festival Pier, a recreational venue where music concerts and other entertainment events are held.

Hotspots on the Water

In the 1980s and 1990s, this part of Delaware Avenue was Philadelphia's hottest nightspot precinct. Its popularity would have been unthinkable even as recently as the 1970s, given that this had been a run-down maritime/business corridor.

At Spring Garden Street

The clubs included: KatManDu, opened in 1991 at Pier 25 North as Philadelphia's first waterfront restaurant-bar, now doing business as Cavanaugh's; Rock Lobster at Pier 15, operating today as Octo Waterfront Grille; Bleachers Sports Club at Spring Garden and Delaware Avenue, later Oasis, then Egypt and then Solo; DECO at Front and Spring Garden; the Eighth Floor at the top floor of a hulking warehouse at Delaware and Poplar, subject of a proposed apartment complex; Kokomo Bay at 927 Delaware, now Bamboo Bar; Aztec Club at 939 Delaware, formerly Baja Beach Club and Chrome and now the Roxxy; Beach Club on Pier 42 North, which had a makeshift sandy beach at its far end and is now part of SugarHouse Casino; and Maui on Pier 53 North near Penn Treaty Park.

Then there's Delilah's Den at Front and Spring Garden. This trendy "gentlemen's club" occupies the site of a Reading Railroad freight warehouse that burned in a tremendous blaze on February 15, 1975. For the ladies, the Cave at Delaware and Fairmount Avenues was billed as the East Coast's number one male revue show. While this "Cave" and this "Den" have nothing to do with the riverside burrows in which Quaker settlers dwelled long ago, they are remarkably close to where some of those caves were located.

These bars and nightclubs became a nuisance to the communities by the water. Public intoxication and other anti-social forms of behavior became the norm for this section of town. More annoying to local dwellers was the nightly fight for street parking.

This is all an example of the conflict between changing uses of the Philadelphia waterfront. The tension between residential and recreational activity came about only once this district became appealing following the end of its use as a commercial and manufacturing zone.

There are even plans afoot to transform a large industrial warehouse at Beach and Richmond Streets into a three-thousand-seat entertainment venue to be operated by Live Nation. The project developer wants to make this the city's premier place to see live music. The warehouse is located in a little-used industrial park in Fishtown, a former manufacturing neighborhood just north of Northern Liberties. Nearby residents are lukewarm to the proposal, as they are concerned that the venue would become yet another rowdy nightclub along the Delaware River.

Most of the nuisance clubs left Columbus Boulevard years ago. Interestingly, though, this part of Philadelphia has had a history of drunkenness and decadence going back to the time of William Penn, as will be shown shortly.

3
Noble to Callowhill

A Romantic Stream Flowing Between a Bloody Lane and a Gallow's Hill

Noble Street may have been named after the early English surveyor Richard Noble. Most of Noble west of Front is gone due to Interstate 95 and urban renewal projects west of the superhighway. The street was known as Bloody Lane in the late 1700s and 1800s because a murder had been committed somewhere along its length.

That the Philadelphia City Morgue was situated on Noble Street for several years after 1870 is unrelated to this. The Reading Railroad in due time acquired and integrated the property into its adjacent rail yard.

Cohoquinoque Creek/Pegg's Run

Pegg's Run was a Delaware River tributary immediately north of Callowhill Street. Originally called the "Cohoquinoque" by local Native Americans, the stream flowed through the southern part of the Northern Liberties District—today the desolate Callowhill East District of Philadelphia. Accounts vary, but Pegg's Run arose around the modern-day intersection of Fifteenth and Spring Garden and was also fed by a spring near Ninth Street.

The navigable Cohoquinoque let farmers convey farm products on flatboats to the Delaware River in order to get to Philadelphia markets. In addition, rowers could make their way far upstream. Young people had many romantic moonlit nights paddling the length of Pegg's Run.

Noble to Callowhill

The creek's later name was derived from Daniel Pegg (ca. 1665–1702), a Quaker brick maker who once possessed much of the Northern Liberties District north of the Cohoquinoque. In 1686, Pegg obtained 350 acres of marshy ground in that region from one Jurian Hartsfielder (ca. 1654–1690), a stray German or Dutchman who held a patent on the territory from the royal governor of New York, Sir Edmund Andros.

The grant for this land, which he called "Hartsfield," dated back six years before William Penn's arrival in America. It was one of the earliest sections of the Delaware River developed by Europeans north of New Sweden, the Swedish colony founded in 1638 along the Delaware, not far from present-day Wilmington, Delaware. In 1655, the Dutch captured the Swedish forts on the river, thus incorporating the Swedish settlements into the Dutch New Netherland colony. This status lasted until the English conquest of the Dutch in 1664 at the start of the Second Anglo-Dutch War. The environs of what became Philadelphia were included in the Charter of Pennsylvania that King Charles II granted to William Penn in 1681.

A bridge was built over Pegg's Run in the 1750s to carry Front Street over the stream. It was termed the "North Bridge" because "North End" was the name given to the territory north of Vine Street in the Northern Liberties District of Philadelphia County. The causeway was also called Poole's Bridge after a man named Poole who had his home and shipyard on a hill a stone's throw away. There were sluices under it to permit the creek to flow freely. The ground on both sides was low and swampy, and quite a few people straying from the bridge died in the mud.

Philadelphia's first manufacturing sector was located along the banks of Pegg's Run, especially textile makers and leather tanneries. The carpet industry in North America began in 1791 nearby along Second Street, as this is where William Peter Sprague started the first commercial carpet mill in the New World (the Philadelphia Carpet Manufactory).

CURVY WILLOW STREET

The North End's industries discharged their offal directly into Pegg's Run for outflow to the Delaware River. The creek thus became tremendously polluted by the late eighteenth century. Public outcry demanded that it be covered over and turned into a sewer, which happened in stages in the early 1800s. However, industries along the way merely obtained entrances into the culvert and continued discharging their waste into the underground stream.

Philadelphia's Lost Waterfront

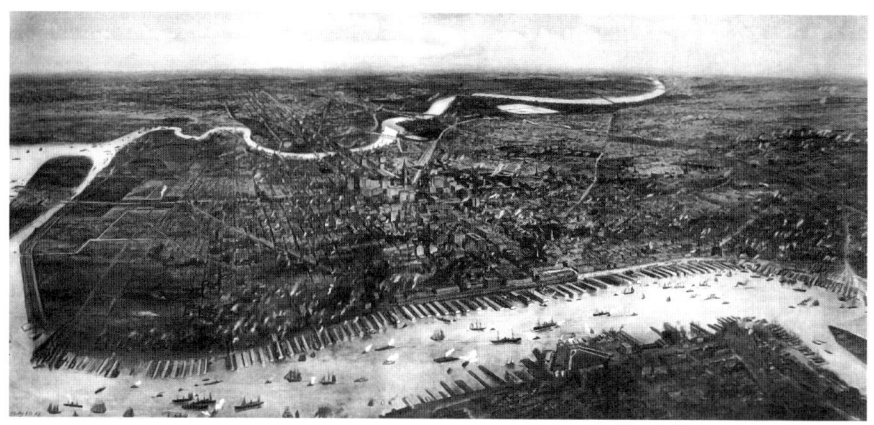

"The Philadelphia of To-Day: The World's Greatest Workshop" (1908), showing the entire central waterfront. *Author's collection.*

The curvilinear Willow Street was built on top of the sewer by 1829. The Northern Liberties and Penn Township Railroad (aka the Delaware and Schuylkill Railroad and the Willow Street Railroad) laid tracks on the surface in 1834. These tracks ran westward from the Willow Street Wharf on the Delaware and connected to the tracks of the Philadelphia and Columbia Railroad on Pennsylvania Avenue west of Broad Street.

In the 1850s, the line became part of the Reading Railroad. The Reading also incorporated the freight houses of the North Pennsylvania Railroad, then located on Front Street between Noble and Willow.

The railroad tracks on Willow Street were removed in the late 1960s as part of the East Callowhill Urban Renewal Area. Hundreds of houses and commercial establishments were torn down in this misguided city planning project that sought to create open space for industrial use. By necessity, the sewer under Willow Street had to remain, which is why Willow Street itself was not eliminated when other streets in the project area were. The sewer still flows to the Delaware at Pier 25, under Cavanaugh's River Deck. Willow Street no longer makes it to Delaware Avenue due to Highway 95.

Curvy Women and Crooked Men by the Delaware

This locale was also Philadelphia's first red-light district. Prostitutes frequented its hostels and boardinghouses, and drinkers gathered at any number of seedy taverns. There were also ramshackle shops and street vendors who

Noble to Callowhill

sold exotic goods taken to them by sailors from ships arriving from all over the world. This commotion attracted a diverse group of people—common laborers, privateers, sailors, gamblers and swindlers of all types.

The area became a center for revelers from Philadelphia and Northern Liberties looking for adventure away from the eyes of authorities. This is because the neighborhood—part of the Northern Liberties District but not Northern Liberties Township—was not fully represented by a municipal government or regularly patrolled by constables until it became part of Philadelphia in 1854. It was that year that the Commonwealth of Pennsylvania combined Northern Liberties and other districts and townships in Philadelphia County into the City of Philadelphia under the Act of Consolidation (P.L. 21, No. 16).

The North End was thus Philadelphia's first "outlaw" district and had a history of violence in the eighteenth century. For instance, Gallow's Hill near Front and Callowhill was the site of a number of public hangings. John Fanning Watson, in his *Annals of Philadelphia and Pennsylvania*, reminisces: "In my youthful days Callowhill street was often called 'Gallows-hill street.'"

The following quote from *Philadelphia and Its Environs: A Guide to the City and Surroundings* (1893) suggests how poorly regarded these parts were by the 1890s and how many people lived and worked in the vicinity:

> *The river-front, northward from the Willow Street freight-yards, is a scene of almost perpetual business movement upon a large scale. Commercial and manufacturing enterprise has here one of its busiest seats. It is not an attractive quarter of the city in its aspect to the stranger, but thousands of wage-earners here obtain subsistence for their families. Great factories seem to be elbowed by lofty warehouses; extensive lumber-yards are flanked by rolling-mills and foundries; and in many of the poorer streets, too often ill-kept and mean, there are battered and weather-worn, old frame houses, and dingy rows of old-fashioned, low, brick dwellings.*

THE WILLOW AND NOBLE STREETS GROUP AND YARDS

The Reading Railroad owned Piers 24, 25 and 27 North, a group of covered finger piers at the bottom of Noble and Willow Streets. The Willow and Noble Streets Group, as it was called, was the second busiest general freight-handling station on the Reading system. These were strictly import piers; the Reading's local export piers were at Port Richmond, a few miles north. Piers

24, 25 and 27 could process sixty-five rail cars of cargo a day, and about five hundred men worked on them in the early 1900s.

The Reading also leased these piers: Pier 24 to the Allan Steamship Company, which operated steamers for freight and passenger traffic between Philadelphia and St. Johns, Halifax, Glasgow and Liverpool; Pier 25 to the Philadelphia Transatlantic Line and the Bull Line, both of which ran steamers for freight to London and Scotland; and Pier 27 to the Holland America and the Scandinavian lines for shipping freight to Rotterdam and Copenhagen.

The Willow and Noble Streets Group worked in conjunction with the Willow and Noble Streets Station on the west side of Delaware Avenue. This was a major railroad freight yard in its day, and a great deal of freight traffic between Philadelphia and New York was exchanged at this point. It's almost certain that the Baldwin Locomotive Works of Philadelphia exported hundreds of steam engines to countries on all continents from this terminal. This harkens back to when Philadelphia was the "Workshop of the World."

Freight movement diminished in the 1950s and ended by the 1970s. A fire destroyed Pier 27 in the morning of August 31, 1972. Firefighters, some on fireboats, worked hard to prevent the blaze from spreading to Piers 25 and 24. They succeeded, but Pier 24 itself burned less than a year later. A dazzling inferno ripped though it on July 7, 1973, leaving the place fully leveled. Arson was suspected in both cases.

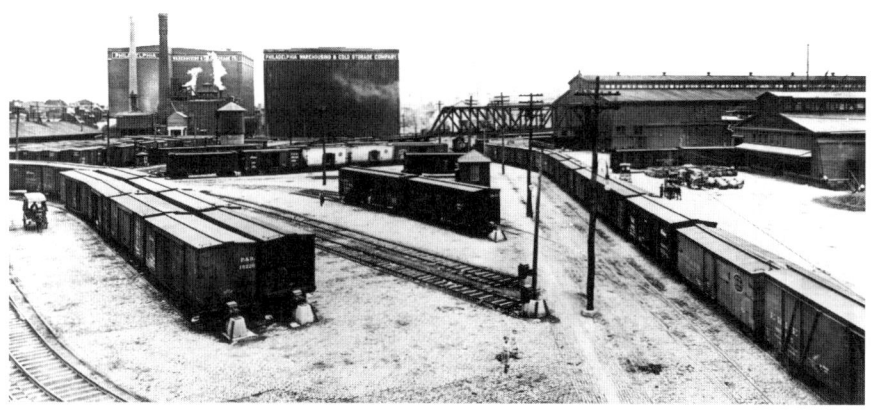

Reading Railroad's Willow and Noble Streets Freight Yard in 1914. Piers 24, 25 and 27 North are on the right. Willow Street is out of the picture on the left. The Philadelphia Cold Storage buildings are in the background. *Philadelphia City Archives.*

Noble to Callowhill

Today, Piers 24 and 27 are parking lots, while Cavanaugh's River Deck is on Pier 25. The Reading Railroad's one-time rail yard is now a land bank currently hosting a self-storage firm. This property has long been touted as the future location of the World Trade Center of Greater Philadelphia. Plans include three office buildings devoted to maritime trade and a residential tower. The goal of this fanciful project is to make Philadelphia one of the one hundred cities in the World Trade Centers Association with a major World Trade Center.

THE TOWN OF CALLOWHILL

Callowhill Street is unusually wide as it approaches the Delaware River because several market sheds were located in the middle of and alongside the avenue in the mid-1700s. A town called Callowhill grew up around this shopping district, having been platted by Thomas Penn, one of William Penn's sons.

Penn's descendants owned much of the land in the Northern Liberties District north of Vine Street, and they routinely sold off lots to generate income. So, about 1768–70, Thomas Penn laid out a north–south lane, New Market Street, between Front and Second and then dedicated four pieces of ground for a public market at each corner of the intersection with Callowhill Street. This became the center of the new town of Callowhill.

Quakers who wanted to get away from the swarming town of Philadelphia moved to Callowhill. It accordingly prospered as the city's most immediate northern suburb. The community remained a food distribution hub and a residential area well after being subsumed into the city of Philadelphia.

Even in the 1950s, when the neighborhood was shabby, Callowhill was still an active meat and produce center. But it was, by then, part of Philadelphia's Skid Row district, a place replete with cheap flophouses, grubby bars, dilapidated warehouses and so on.

When Interstate 95 plowed through this quarter, it completely obliterated what had once been Callowhill. The bustling town, centered at the intersection that William Penn's son established, was located exactly where Callowhill Street dips under the multilane freeway. Today, not even the shadow of a trace of the town of Callowhill exists.

4

Callowhill to Vine

Penn's Surviving Steps and Ships and Ferries on the Frozen Delaware

Callowhill Street was first called "the new street" since it was the first road opened in Northern Liberties, north of Philadelphia's original northern limit. This was in 1690. William Penn later renamed the street after his second wife, Hannah Callowhill (1671–1726), apparently during his second stay in America (1701–02).

The Wood Street Steps

The steps at 323 North Front Street are usually referred to as the Wood Street Steps. This staircase consists of fourteen granite blocks, including twelve treads and two landing areas. They are the last set of William Penn's public stairs along the Philadelphia bank of the Delaware River to survive.

That they do survive is a miracle of sorts. As late as the 1980s, the Wood Street Steps were in jeopardy. An adjoining owner wanted the city to strike the passageway from the street plan so that he could acquire the ground to enlarge his property. The River's Edge Civic Association, a local civic group, put a stop to that plan.

The stairway was once an extension of a slender alley between Vine and Callowhill called Wood Street. The steps were built between 1702 and 1737, but while the treads originally could have been wooden, there's some evidence that the granite steps there today may date from

Callowhill to Vine

the late seventeenth century. The stone treads were there for sure in 1737, when Wood Street was first registered as a public street.

The ten-foot-wide passageway between 321 and 325 North Front—and between 322 and 324 North Water—is still labeled as Wood in city records and is administered by the Philadelphia Department of Streets. The Wood Street Steps were certified by the city's Historical Commission in 1986 and are listed on the Philadelphia Register of Historic Places.

A land warrant (patent) by William Penn to one Henry Johnson in March 1689 actually established the Wood Street Steps. Johnson was the buyer of forty feet of ground on the east side of Front Street north of Vine. A provision reads:

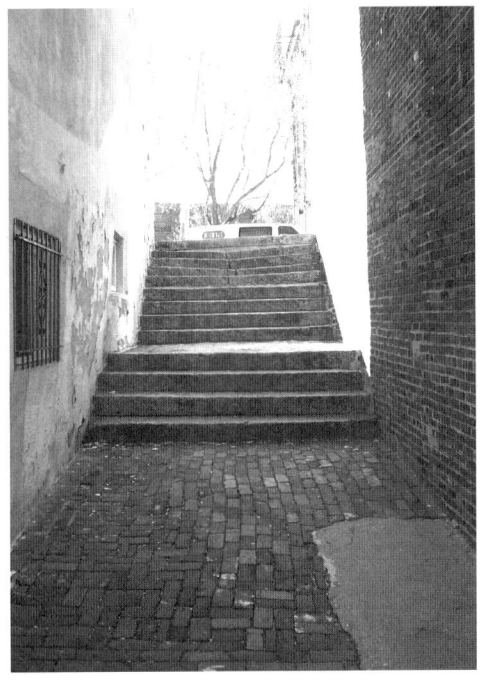

The Wood Street Steps today. *Photo by the author.*

> [T]*he said Henry Johnson his Heirs and Assigns shall further leave a Proportionable Part of the said Lot for Building one publick Pair of Stone Stairs of ten Foot in Bredth leading from the said Front Street down to the said Lower Street or Cartway and so forward to the Wharfs And one Pair of Stone Stairs from off the Wharfs down to Low Water Mark of the said River in the Middle or most convenient place between Vine Street and the North Bridge.*

This passage substantiates the authorization of stone steps back to William Penn himself, although it doesn't prove if and when any steps were built. It also indicates that the Wood Street Steps were initially meant to be made of stone. Local historians have generally thought that this and other bank stairs were made of wood until the 1720s or 1730s, at which time granite steps were installed. The warrant shows that Penn wanted stone rather than wooden steps and makes it more likely that the existing Wood Street Steps were built prior to earlier estimated dates.

The warrant also directs that the riverbank stairs between Vine and Callowhill were to extend down into the Delaware River at low tide on the east side of Water Street (the "Lower Street" or "Cartway"). It's unclear if these particular steps ever reached into the Delaware, but other bank stairways did continue on the east side of Water Street as walkways with additional stairs that descended straight into the river for use at low tide. (Yes, the Delaware is a tidal waterway, rising and falling about six feet twice a day.)

Four treads of the Wood Street Steps have cracked in half and are sagging as a result of subsidence. River's Edge Civic Association is planning to repair the steps and conduct an archaeological investigation beneath them. The group also wants to draw attention to this and all the Penn stairwells via the installation of a Pennsylvania State Historical Marker.

SHIPBUILDING (I OF III): THE WEST SHIPYARD/HERTZ LOT

Wood Street got its name from timber being carted along it to a handful of eighteenth-century shipyards fronting the Delaware River in the vicinity of Vine Street. Indeed, under the parking lots approximately in front of the Wood Street Steps are the remains of the West Shipyard, one of four local yards fabricating fishing craft, riverboats and oceangoing vessels.

James West (?–1701) set up his yard on the west bank of the river as early as 1676, years before the arrival of William Penn in America. In the days before dry docks, sailing ships needing repair would be dragged up slipways (launching ramps) to enable repairs to be made. New vessels, needless to say, were also built on such ramps. A ropeyard was immediately north of the West Shipyard.

After West's death in 1701, his son took over and developed the shipyard into a miniature "company town," complete with shops and inns to support its workers. But the yard became less useful as ships became both larger and equipped with steam engines driving propellers and paddle wheels—hauling ships ashore was no longer practical. The West Shipyard had faded from the scene by the early 1800s, and the old slipways and quays were filled in (again, made-earth) as Philadelphia's waterfront was pressed farther east into the Delaware.

Disturbances at this site were relatively minor because the structures built there—a coal yard, a fruit warehouse, the Vine Street Market, etc.—did not

Callowhill to Vine

have deep foundations. By the early 1900s, a rail yard of the Reading Railroad covered the block. Now topped by a parking lot across from Pier 19, the West Shipyard may be the last intact vestige of Philadelphia's colonial port heritage.

A small archaeological dig was carried out in 1987 at part of the plot encompassing the West site. (The ground is identified as the Hertz Lot from the car rental firm previously in business there.) Among the findings were the remnants of eighteenth-century wharves and a slipway, all in good condition. The dig was filled and paved over afterward to keep it preserved. This was the first archaeological site on the Philadelphia Register of Historic Places.

The Hertz Lot slipway is the only feature of its kind unearthed in excavations on the East Coast. Since the West Shipyard escaped the havoc wrought by Interstate 95, there is undoubtedly much valuable material buried not far underground. A dig here may yield a fine record of the parcel's uses from 1676 until recent times. Plans for such an excavation are in the works.

PENNY POT TAVERN AND LANDING

The bowsprits of ships at West's yard almost reached the eaves of buildings on Water Street. One of these was the Penny Pot Tavern. West bought this well-known landmark from a widow in 1689 or 1690. As specified by Watson, it was situated three houses north of the northwest corner of Vine and Water. The tavern was a two-story brick structure with its front facing south.

The renowned Penny Pot Tavern was allowed to sell beer for "a penny a pot" (or quart), as per the Duke of York's decree in 1682. It was therefore

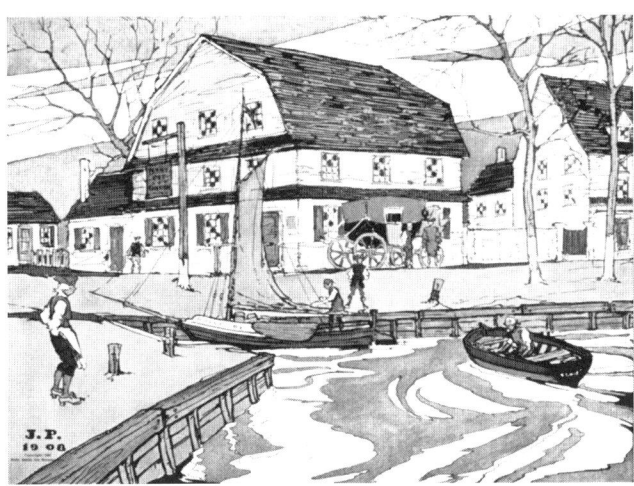

The Penny Pot Tavern and its adjacent landing at Vine Street. *Library of Congress.*

a place where beer could be bought for about half the price of most other brew houses.

The saloon became the Jolly Tar Inn after 1800 and was later incorporated into the Rising Sun Hotel next door. The Penny Pot building burned in a fire that destroyed the entire block in 1850 (discussed later). The edifice currently on the site contains a quarter-sized facsimile of the tavern on the roof. Best seen from Front Street, it was erected by the architect who moved there in the 1970s.

The Penny Pot Landing, built by James West, was basically in front of the inn, between his shipyard and the Vine Street Landing. The two ultimately became one and the same.

Vine Street Landing and Ferry

Vine Street was originally called Valley Street since a ravine or vale led to the Delaware River there. This is why a boat landing was to be found at this point even before William Penn's era; the valley offered easy access into the region's interior. Hunters and traders from settled territories in New Jersey had crossed the channel there throughout the 1600s to get to the bountiful lands of what became Pennsylvania.

Penn had first dedicated the Vine Street Landing for public use in 1683. He further proclaimed in his "Charter of Privileges" for inhabitants of Pennsylvania (1701) that "the Landing-places now and heretofore used at the Penny-pot-house and Blue-anchor... shall be left open and common for the Use and Service of the said City and all others." Penn wanted to prevent some enterprising Philadelphian from buying the rights to these boat landings, which he intended for public use indefinitely.

The Vine Street Landing was one of the busiest ferry landings on the Delaware. In the early 1700s, it primarily serviced the Upper Ferry (otherwise known as "Uncle Billy's Ferry") operated by William Cooper. The Cooper's Point Ferry, a more formal venture, took over this route and later became associated with the Camden and Atlantic Railroad. Eventually taken over by the Pennsylvania Railroad, that rail line ran trains to Atlantic City and other shore resorts.

Cooper's Point Ferry billed itself as "Philadelphia's Front Door to Atlantic City." Countless Philadelphians boarded ferryboats at Pier 16 North to get to the line's Camden (New Jersey) terminal, where they would board trains that would take them to the seaside for a few days of relaxation.

Callowhill to Vine

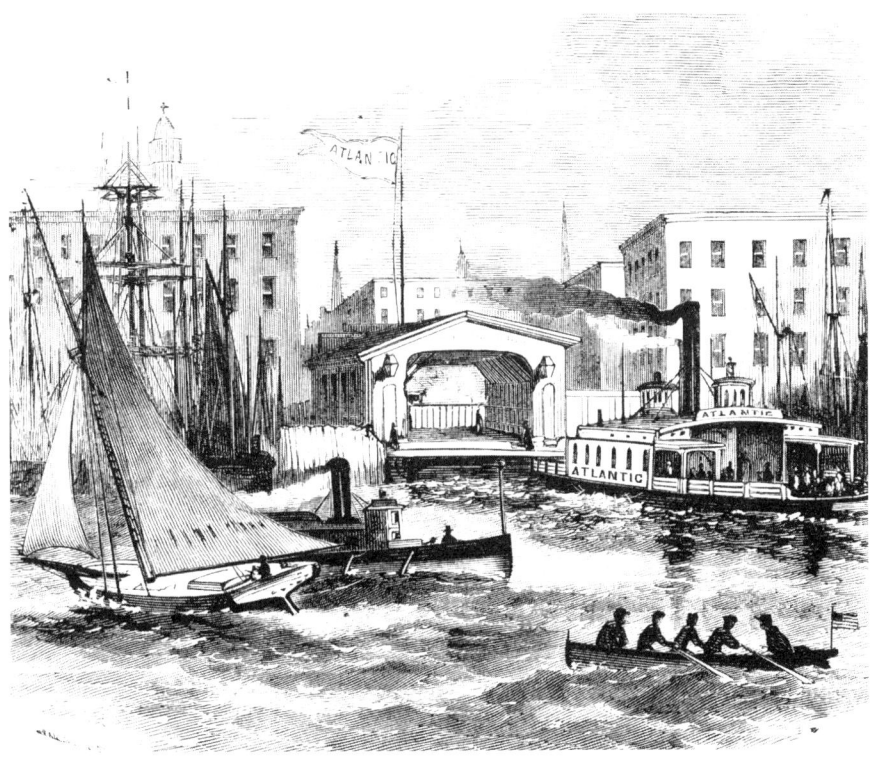

An 1875 view of the Vine Street Landing and Ferry. *Adam Levine Collection.*

When it went out of business in 1926 or so, the Vine Street Ferry was reputed to be the oldest ferry service in America, operating continuously for more than two hundred years.

FERRIES CROSSING THE DELAWARE (I OF II)

The Vine Street Landing was not unique. A public boat/ferry landing was at the base of every east–west street in Philadelphia's younger years. The ferries allowed people to cross the Delaware in the days before the Benjamin Franklin Bridge provided the first Philadelphia crossing. They transported travelers, shoppers and day-trippers from Philadelphia and Camden and from points all over. Some boats were powered by horses driving a paddle wheel—horse-boats. Oarsmen propelled others.

Then came the Industrial Revolution. The factories, shops, stores and offices of both Philadelphia and Camden employed hundreds of thousands of workers, and some of them lived or worked on the opposite side of the river. So they had to take a ferry trip twice daily. To meet the demand, steam-powered ferries plied the Delaware by the middle of the 1800s.

SHIPBUILDING (II OF III): OVERSEAS TRADE AND THE AMERICAN CLYDE

Other boats—first sailing ships and then steamships—would take people to Bristol, Burlington, Trenton, Chester, Wilmington, Baltimore and so forth. Ships sailing to England, the West Indies, China, India and other remote destinations routinely left from the city's Delaware waterfront in the 1700s and 1800s. Philadelphia merchants were known in the "counting houses" of the far corners of the world from the 1790s to the 1850s.

A group of Philadelphia and New York merchants had equipped the first American ship to sail to China. The *Empress of China* left New York City on February 22, 1784, and landed in Canton that August 28. The ship returned in 1785 with a full load of silks, porcelain, spices and tea, thus starting the American-China trade.

Also in 1784, the first American ship to visit India departed Philadelphia on March 24. The *United States* was outfitted by a group of Philadelphian merchants and reached the city of Pondicherry later in 1784. Eight years later, the brigantine *Philadelphia* was the first American ship to visit Australia—as well as perhaps the first foreign trade vessel ever to visit Australia. Plus, the frigate *John* left Philadelphia to become the first American ship to visit South America, arriving at the present capital of Uruguay in 1798.

Many of these vessels were made in shipyards up and down the Delaware River. The Delaware was even nicknamed the "American Clyde" because it rivaled Europe's great shipbuilding region on Scotland's Clyde River. Ship fabrication firms included Neafie & Levy, John Roach & Sons, Simpson & Neill, Bireley, Hillman & Co. and William Cramp & Sons. James West's yard was part of the progression of this industry, as was that of Joshua Humphreys, discussed in chapter sixteen.

Philadelphia's shipyards became vast operations as ships transitioned from sail to steam power and from wooden to iron hulls. Local shipyards set records for physical plant and production during the heyday of American shipbuilding around World War I. Hundreds of thousands of workers were employed in building ships and in related maritime industries on both banks

Callowhill to Vine

of the Delaware. This concentration of shipyards was the largest shipbuilding industry in the world.

Alas, the building and repairing of ships is no longer a major industry in Philadelphia. The last machine shop of Cramp Shipyard—one of several structures of a thirty-acre compound in the city's Kensington district—was demolished in early 2011. Why? To build a new I-95 interchange, but of course.

THE FROZEN DELAWARE

From the Vine Street Landing and other places that offered easy access to the Delaware, people would skate on the iced-over river during the many times it froze in the eighteenth and nineteenth centuries. Skating early on became a sport in which Philadelphians were noted, possibly because Quaker leaders approved of this ostensibly frivolous pursuit.

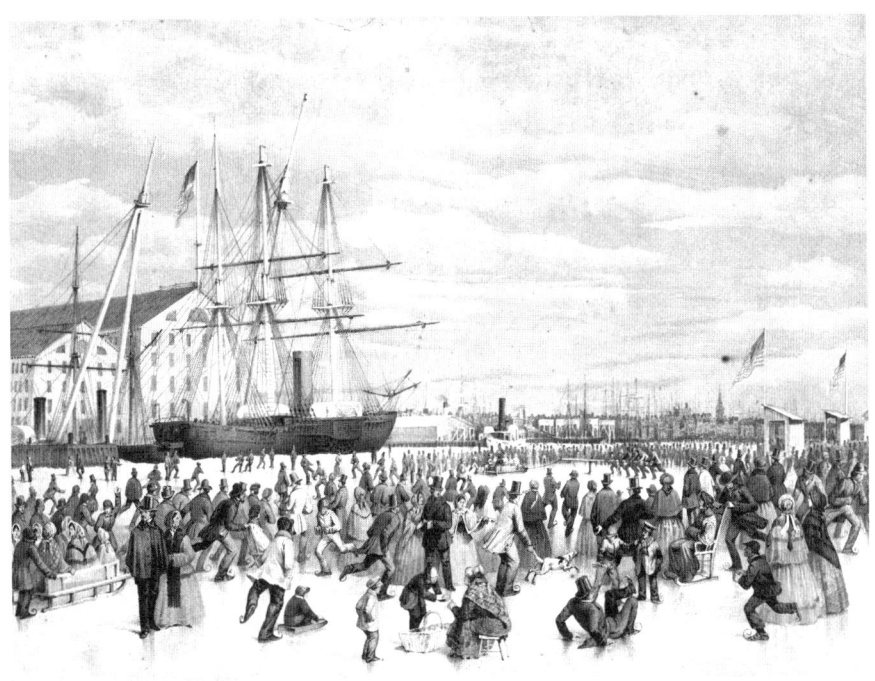

Ice-skating on the frozen Delaware in the winter of 1856, near the first Philadelphia Naval Yard. This is an image of one of several instances of such a scene in the 1800s. *Library of Congress.*

Watson describes the scene vividly. On days the Delaware was frozen, booths were put up to sell refreshments to the gathered crowd; sometimes an ox roast would add to the excitement. Horses were also specially shod for racing sleighs on the solid river, and the course would go miles upstream. The ice could get so thick—often more than two feet—that horses pulled loaded ferryboats across the channel atop the ice!

It's no wonder that the first icebreaker in the world was built for Philadelphia in 1837 to keep traffic moving on the Delaware during winter months. Christened *City Ice Boat No. 1*, this was the first of a local fleet of such ships. Its original steam engine was made by Philadelphia's Matthias Baldwin, who later won fame for his railroad locomotives. *City Boat 1* cost $70,000 to build and remained in service for eighty years.

Pier 19 North (the Vine Street Pier)

In 1907, the Pennsylvania legislature and the City of Philadelphia established the Department of Wharves, Docks and Ferries as a division of the Philadelphia Department of Commerce. The new port authority replaced the Board of Port Wardens, which had regulated Philadelphia's harbor activities and maintained its wharf line since 1766.

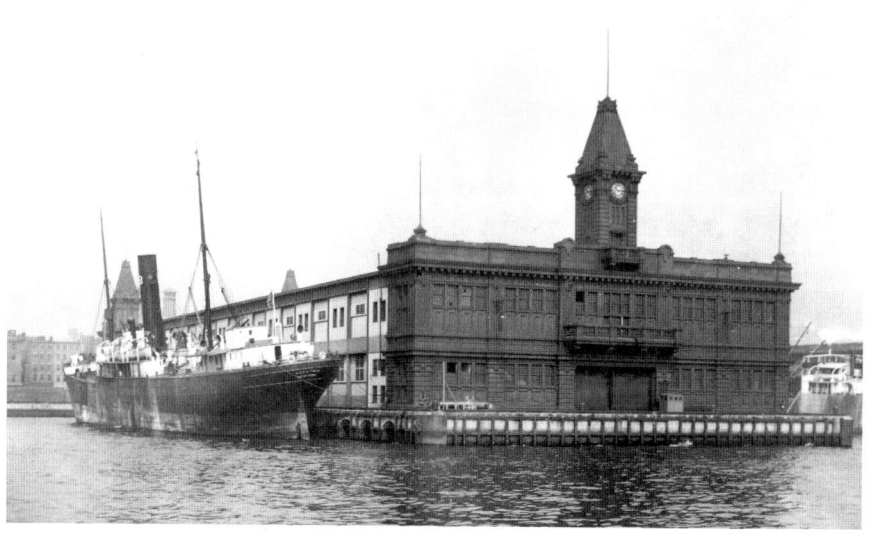

Pier 19 North from the water, September 9, 1919. Dave & Busters occupies this pier today, along with a Japanese restaurant at the far end. *Philadelphia City Archives.*

Callowhill to Vine

Given broad regulatory power to condemn and improve the city's waterfront, the Department of Wharves promptly began construction of a series of municipally owned piers and other port facilities along the Delaware. The first of these was Pier 19 North between Vine and Callowhill. The city built this, the Vine Street Pier, in 1911 as a 571-foot-long, double-decked structure with an exposed steel superstructure.

At one time the biggest pier in Philadelphia, Pier 19 was first leased to the Philadelphia & Gulf Steamship Company, a firm engaged in passenger and freight service to southern ports. The city also leased the Vine Street Pier to the Italia Line, which brought immigrant-laden ships from Italy to America.

Pier 19 is better known today as Dave & Busters, a dining and entertainment center that opened in 1994. Few people who go there for food and fun know that the building was once a municipal immigration station that processed thousands and thousands of Italian immigrants.

EATING BY THE WATER

Other dining venues along Delaware Avenue today include: Hibachi Japanese Steakhouse at the far (river) end of Pier 19, formerly Meiji-En; Cavanaugh's River Deck at 417 North Columbus Boulevard; Octo Waterfront Grille at 221 North Columbus; Ristorante La Veranda, an Italian eatery in the head house between Piers 3 and 5; Keating's River Grill at the Hyatt Penn's Landing; *Spirit of Philadelphia* and *Philadelphia Belle*, both offering lunch and dinner cruises; Chart House Philadelphia, a longtime restaurant at Penn's Landing Marina; and *Moshulu*, a South Seas eatery aboard the world's oldest four-masted sailing ship.

Some folks, men in particular, will remember the Hooters of Penn's Landing at the foot of Callowhill Street. This place opened in the mid-1990s on a hundred-year-old ferryboat. Hooters closed in 2002, and the ferry sank into the mud after it was abandoned. It was raised in 2005 and then scuttled off Cape May as an artificial reef.

And old-timers may recall the Riverfront Restaurant and Dinner Theater. It opened in 1974—very early in the waterfront's rebirth—and closed in 1993. The site is now part of the Waterfront Square Condominium complex.

5

THE RIVERFRONT CAVES OF PRIMITIVE PHILADELPHIA

Striving to endure the dawn of their new lives in the New World, pioneering Quakers lived in man-made caves dug into the muddy bank of the Delaware River. Early settlers wintered in these caves in 1681; about one-third of Philadelphia's population was living underground the following year. The grottos were often on riverbank land that the newcomers had acquired or hoped to acquire from the Pennsylvania Proprietary.

CAVES?

The caves sheltered these stalwart men and women of the Religious Society of Friends (Quakers) while they built their homes close by or farther inland. In some cases, the settlers may have been trying to stake a claim to an advantageous spot on the riverbank at which they hoped to build a house. (Dubbed "bank houses," the dwellings built on the bank lots were among the first homes constructed in Philadelphia.) As Watson tells it:

> *Most Philadelphians have had some vague conceptions of the caves and cabins in which the primitive settlers made their temporary residence. The caves were generally formed by digging into the ground, near the verge of the*

The Riverfront Caves of Primitive Philadelphia

river-front bank, about three feet in depth; thus, making half their chamber under ground, and the remaining half above ground was formed of sods of earth, or earth and brush combined. The roofs were formed of layers of limbs, or split pieces of trees, over-laid with sod or bark, river rushes, &c. The chimneys were of stones and river pebbles, mortared together with clay and grass, or river reeds.

The local Delaware Indians had long used such hollows by the river for temporary winter shelter. They told the Quakers that the holes had been created by muskrats and were then enlarged for human use.

Settlers constructed some of the caves by burrowing horizontally into the high bank of the Delaware. Other caves were made by digging down three or four feet deep atop the bank and then building a wall of earth a yard high around the excavation, thus forming a chamber half above and half below ground. The roofs were made of layers of limbs or logs covered with sod or bark and thatched with straw or river rushes. Most of these hollows had chimneys consisting of stones fixed with mortar.

John Faris in *The Romance of Old Philadelphia* (1918) provides additional details:

Many of the first colonists were compelled to put up with rude cave houses, built in the sloping ground above the Delaware. These could not have been very different from the sod houses on the prairies or the potato cellars still to be found on many farms. A bank formed the back of the house, while timbers were driven into the ground for the sides and the front. Earth was heaped against the side timbers, a door and a window or two were cut, and a roof of timbers covered with earth completed the whole. The window aperture contained a sliding board which, when closed, shut out some of the cold as well as the light. Sometimes a bladder or isinglass [mica] was stretched across. Those who were able to display a small paned window were proud of the achievement and were looked on with envy by their neighbors.

Watson recounts that the Coats family, Quaker brick makers, lived in a cave at the southwest corner of Front and Green in Northern Liberties. They preserved their little grotto as the cellar of the house they raised at that spot. It stood until about 1830.

Cave-Born John Key

John Key (1682–1767) came into the world on July 20, 1682, in a shallow cave on top of which the Penny Pot Tavern was later built. The first English child born in Philadelphia County (and the second or third born in all of Pennsylvania), he lived a long life in primal Pennsylvania. Benjamin Franklin reported the news of Key's death in the *Pennsylvanian Gazette* on July 16, 1767:

> *At Kennet, in Chester County, the 5th instant, died John Key, in the 85th year of his age, and the next day was interred in the burial place belonging to the people called Quakers, in that township, attended by a large number of reputable people, his neighbours and acquaintance. He was born in a cave (near the Delaware River), long afterwards known by the name of Penny-Pot, near Race-street, and William Penn, our first proprietor, gave him a lot of ground, as a compliment on his being the first child born in this city.*

The Spacious Lair of Francis Daniel Pastorius

The most famous denizen of these riverside hovels was Francis Daniel Pastorius (1651–1720), the German scholar and lawyer who came to America in 1683. He was the agent of a group of German investors—the German Society, aka the Frankfort Company—who were interested in procuring land from William Penn. Pastorius did so and founded the community of Germantown, where he went to live in 1685. (An ardent abolitionist, he drafted the first protest against slavery in America there; the town is now part of Philadelphia.)

Before leaving for Germantown, Francis Pastorius lived in an elaborate cave somewhere near modern-day Front and Lombard. It was located on one of three bank lots that Penn sold to the German Society, together with tracts in Philadelphia County and fifteen thousand acres elsewhere in Pennsylvania. The following is from Pastorius's description of the bank lots and his earthen abode, from a letter written on March 7, 1684, and reproduced in *The Settlement of Germantown* (1899):

> [The three lots] *lie thus along the Delaware, for it is a wide street* [Front], *upon which follows our first lot, one hundred feet wide and four hundred long, at the end of which comes a street, then our second lot, also of the same width and length. Further another street and then our third lot.*

The Riverfront Caves of Primitive Philadelphia

Thus there can be built upon each one two houses in front, and two behind, directly alongside of each other, in all twelve houses upon the three lots, with their courts, properly, all of which front upon the street etc.

I have already upon the first, together with our servant put up a little house one-half under the earth and half above, which is indeed only thirty feet long, and fifteen broad, but when the people from Crefeld were lodging with me, it could accommodate twenty persons. Upon the window made of oiled paper, over the door I wrote, Parva Domus sed arnica bonis procul este profani! [A little house, but a friend to the good: keep away, ye profane!] —*which W. Penn read not long ago and was pleased with. Besides this I dug a cellar seven feet deep, twelve wide, and twenty long, on the Delaware stream.*

The thirteen original settlers of Germantown drew lots for their new homes at this place on October 25, 1683.

In 1924, members of the Site and Relic Society of Germantown and the Pennsylvania Historical Commission placed a tablet on a wall at 502 South Front Street to commemorate Pastorius's connection to that spot. The tablet is long gone, as is the house. Newer housing is on the west side of Front nowadays. The Delaware Expressway is on the east side.

DEBAUCHERY IN THE GROTTOS

The settlers often operated unlicensed taverns and other businesses in their embankment chambers. These places were the scene of illicit activity of all kinds. Gambling dens and brothels flourished. When families vacated the burrows for better housing, new families—or gamblers or prostitutes—usually moved in. Watson continues:

In 1685, the Grand Jury present Joseph Knight, for suffering drunkenness and evil orders in his cave; and several drinking houses to debauch persons are also presented. They also present all the empty caves that do stand in the Front street, "which is to be 60 feet wide," wherefore, the court orders that they forthwith "be pulled down," by the constables, and "demolished."

How did William Penn feel about all this? The *Minutes of the Board of Property of the Province of Pennsylvania* (1893) disclose that he issued a "Proclamation Concerning the Caves of Philadelphia" in 1686 while he was in England:

Philadelphia's Lost Waterfront

> *Whereas I did at first, in regard of the infancy of things and specially out of tenderness to the poorer sort, permit divers Caves to be made in the Bank of Philadelphia fronting Delaware River, for a present accommodation, and perceiving that they are commonly disposed of from one to another as a kind of Property, and taking farther notice of the great Detriment that is like to insue to the* [Front] *Street by the continuation of them, as well as the Disorders that their great Secresy hath given occasion to loose People to commit in them, I do hereby desire and strictly order and warne all the Inhabitants of the said Caves to depart the same within two Months after the Publication hereof.*

Still, enforcement was difficult, as the following 1687 entry in the *Minutes of the Board of Property* attests:

> *David Lloyd, ye attorney General, according to Request, in the forenoon met the Commissiones, they consulted about a Method to prosecute those who would not go quietly out of their Caves, it was the attorney's opinion to prosecute them for a Nusance. It was ordered y't ye Messenger should go to*

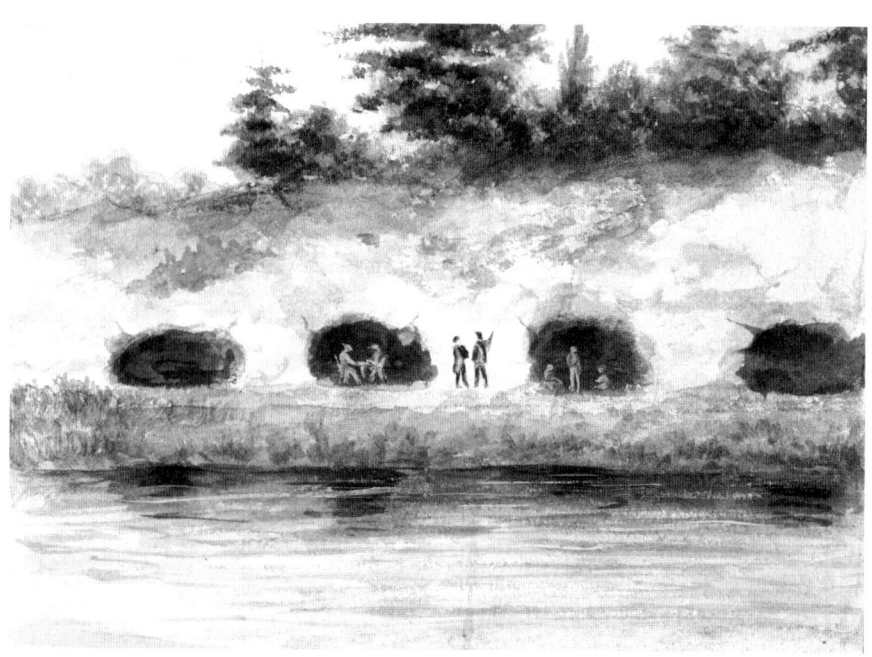

The 1680s caves along the Delaware River, as imagined by painter William Breton. *The Library Company of Philadelphia.*

The Riverfront Caves of Primitive Philadelphia

Every respective Cave and warn ye Inhabitants to depart the same within one Week, and those that did not should be prosecuted accordingly.

Ultimately, the forbidden grottos emptied. Some were filled in, while others became part of the basements of houses and stores that were built between Front and Water Streets, right on top of the caves. (The width of the strip of ground between Front and Water from Pegg's Run to Pine Street ranged between twenty-five and forty-one feet but was usually forty feet.) Yet others were converted into arched vaults under the east pavement of Front Street and then connected to newly dug basements.

LEGACY OF THE RIVERFRONT CAVES

The buildings on Front between Vine and Callowhill represent the last bank houses of Philadelphia. While the actual structures may have changed, the historic property lines (generally denoted by party walls) in many cases remain unchanged and go back hundreds of years. All these structures were built after 1850, most using the foundations of buildings destroyed in the terrible conflagration on the Philadelphia waterfront that year (discussed in chapter seven).

But their basements—some under Front Street's east sidewalk—may date back to the riverbank caves dug out by courageous Quakers in the 1680s. It is fortunate that a group of urban pioneers came to the block in the 1970s and resuscitated what had been a row of derelict storefronts and warehouses. In doing so, they preserved what are maybe the oldest man-made (or muskrat-made?) things in Philadelphia. Today's residents use these chambers as storage closets, wine cellars and exercise rooms.

In short, Front Street between Vine and Callowhill corresponds to the last unbroken segment of the Delaware River shoreline since William Penn's time. It's a remnant of Philadelphia's waterfront that has not been devastated by the forces of commerce, industry and transportation.

And what a narrow escape this block had—not once, but twice! It eluded its demise for the Delaware Expressway in the 1970s and then dodged another bullet when the Vine Street Expressway (I-676/U.S. 30) connected to I-95 in the 1980s. Interstate 676 opened in 1991 after years of planning, controversy and construction. Its high-flying ramps did away with many city blocks to the west.

6

FRONT STREET

Pennsylvania's First Street and a Kingly Highway

Front Street's initial name was "Delaware Front Street," and it was called that well into the 1800s. (A Schuylkill Front Street was planned for the Schuylkill River's east bank; it wound up as Twenty-second Street.) Front Street takes the place of what could or should be "First Street" in Philadelphia, just as Broad Street takes the place of "Fourteenth Street."

Laid out atop the Delaware's western embankment when Penn's settlement was platted, Front Street was the first street surveyed and built in Pennsylvania. It hugged the river north and south of Philadelphia and became the town's principal thoroughfare during and after the colonial period.

Delaware Front Street was first a residential street with commanding houses facing the river from its western side. It then turned into a commercial corridor with shops, storehouses and boardinghouses. "Front street was the former great street for all kinds of goods by wholesale," John Watson stated.

The King's Highway

Front Street was the main road to Pennsylvania settlements along the Delaware, the town of Frankford above all. Revolutionary War armies, both American and British, used it as the primary entrance into Philadelphia from the north. Right before the Battle of Brandywine, the Continental army marched into the city via Front and then turned west onto Chestnut

Front Street

Street to head out of town. The only way to get into or out of Philadelphia during the city's 1777–78 occupation was to pass through the military post at Front and Noble.

All this stems from Front Street being part of the King's Highway, a road that followed an old Indian trail along the river's west bank from New Castle, Delaware, to the falls of the Delaware at Trenton, New Jersey. The Provincial Council of Pennsylvania ordered construction of this, the first major highway in Pennsylvania, in 1686.

The King's Highway (aka Kingshighway) reached New York City via central New Jersey by 1756, thus creating the key colonial link between Philadelphia and New York. It later became the first direct stagecoach route between the two cities and reduced travel time between them to three days. The King's Highway would eventually extend north and south along the East Coast through several states. It still exists as U.S. Route 13, following closely its original configuration and paralleling Interstate 95.

Front Street Today

The construction of Highway 95 resulted in the crude relocation and narrowing of Front Street from Race to Arch and its elimination between Vine and Race. This was a callous act to inflict on a historic street that had once been so critical to Philadelphia as a whole, as well as its bygone settlers and merchants and the great William Penn personally.

Front Street north of Vine does retain some of its early appearance, old-time Belgian blocks and all. It even rises and falls a bit from Vine to Spring Garden, especially as it heads past the former location of Pegg's Run. This is a manifestation, to this day, of the rolling terrain of the original high bluff on the Delaware River's edge. Front Street south of Arch is paved with asphalt, but it, too, undulates, particularly as it approaches where Dock Creek used to be.

Since 2000, several new or rehabbed apartment and condominium complexes have cropped up on the west side of Front Street between Arch and Walnut. The modern high-rises near Walnut Street are out of scale and style with the older buildings of Old City and Society Hill Philadelphia, but they offer terrific views of the Delaware and exemplify the renewed allure of Front Street as a residential address.

7

VINE TO RACE

A Calamitous Blaze and a Colossal Bridge

To reiterate, Vine Street was originally called Valley Street since a ravine dipped toward the Delaware in this vicinity.

WILLIAM RUSH'S STUDIO

The studio of William Rush (1756–1833) was once on the west side of Front Street between Vine and Race Streets. The son of a ship's carpenter, he was the first native-born sculptor in America and is acclaimed as the "Father of American Sculpture."

Rush began his career as a maker of figureheads for ships, which is doubtlessly why he set up shop so close to the Delaware. Usually nine feet tall, his figureheads were the first to give an idea of life and motion to that type of work. His carvings were always wood; he never worked with stone. Rush evolved from a carver of figureheads into the creator of the first monumental American sculptures, *Comedy* and *Tragedy* (1808).

William Rush's concern for civic improvement and his work on public buildings anticipated the direction public art would take in America. His workhouse is gone, lost in the fire described below. Even the block of Front Street on which his shop stood is gone, that locale having been taken over for I-95.

Vine to Race

GREAT CONFLAGRATION OF 1850

The spectacular waterfront conflagration on July 9, 1850, was the first great fire in Philadelphia's history and the city's most destructive inferno during the nineteenth century. It started at a five-story warehouse on the east side of Water Street, between Vine and Race, at what is approximately 237 North Water these days.

The fire began when pressed hay stored in an upper floor of the storehouse somehow combusted. This itself did not cause much alarm, but a number of violent explosions of saltpeter—stored in the warehouse's basement—spread the fire. Burning hay and flaming embers from the blown-up building flew in all directions. Summer winds conveyed bits of smoldering sulfur (stored in an adjoining storehouse) all the way to Broad Street.

Very quickly, the ensuing fire reached southward to Race Street, westward to Second and northward past Callowhill. People who lived close by packed their things and prepared for a sudden evacuation. The city was at risk of a cataclysm that night. Mass confusion prevailed. The light of the fire was seen for thirty miles around.

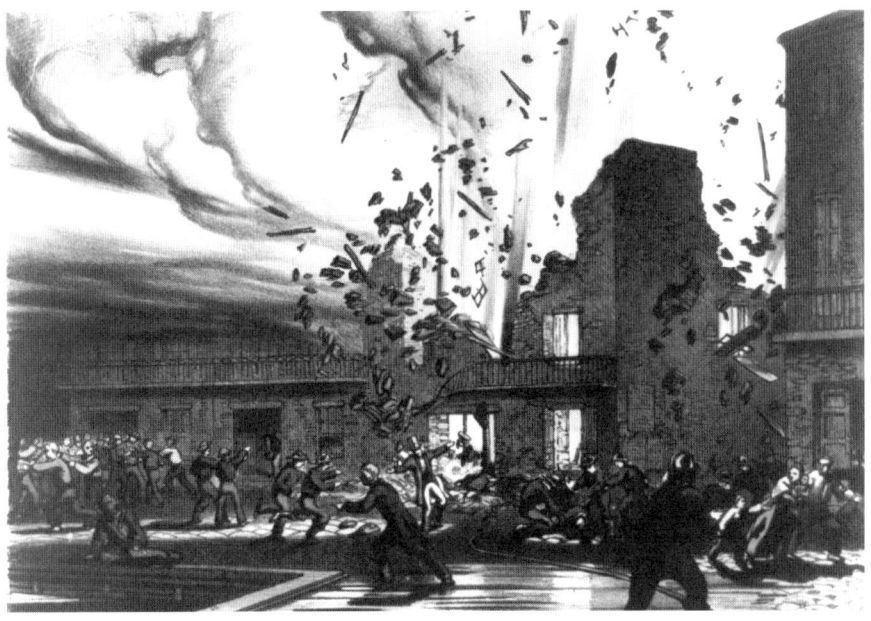

An exciting print: "The Great Conflagration in Philadelphia on Tuesday, July 9th, 1850." *Library of Congress.*

News of the blaze was telegraphed across the United States and was even later reported in Great Britain. More than one hundred firemen from New York City, Newark, Wilmington and Baltimore arrived by express train to relieve Philadelphia firefighters who had became exhausted by their exertions and the heat. This was probably the first American disaster in which technology—telegraphs and trains—were employed.

The fire happened a few years before the 1854 Consolidation of Philadelphia, so the congested commercial area was partly outside the city's original northern limit at Vine Street. Half of the zone of devastation was thus in Northern Liberties.

The inferno was subdued sometime during the night. At least twenty-eight lives were lost (accounts vary), including some killed in the street and in adjacent buildings as a consequence of the initial explosion. Others were trampled in the chaos. Yet others drowned in the Delaware River from the shock of the explosion or from purposefully jumping into the river to flee the calamity. Several firemen died, too.

Newspaper articles reported that 367 buildings were reduced to ashes within some eighteen acres. Roughly 300 of the burned structures were small row homes, leaving dozens of working-class families homeless. In a fairly uncommon civic action in that era, the Philadelphia City Councils appropriated $10,000 for the relief of survivors, and the Commissioners of Northern Liberties did the same. Local citizens also contributed some $31,000 to help the injured victims.

The city block that was ground zero of the explosion and fire was rebuilt and resumed being as overcrowded as before. An empty lot now occupies the block. Plans for a condominium development there fell through, but it seems likely that this lot will one day be used for residential or recreational purposes, given its favorable location.

The Delaware River (Benjamin Franklin) Bridge

Leaders from Pennsylvania and New Jersey had talked for years about constructing a bridge or tunnel between Philadelphia and Camden. In 1919, legislation was passed in both states to build a bridge across the Delaware River. The study of right of ways proposed for the span entailed one of the first traffic surveys in America. Potential Philadelphia endpoints included Washington Square, Sixth and Spring Garden and even Third and Market.

Vine to Race

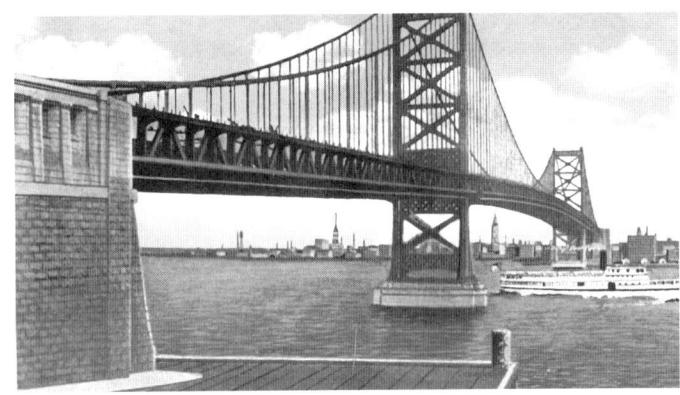

The Benjamin Franklin Bridge, looking toward Philadelphia. This large undated postcard was produced for the Sesquicentennial International Exposition of 1926. *Author's collection.*

Construction of the Delaware River Bridge began on January 6, 1922, and it opened on July 1, 1926, just in time for the nation's Sesquicentennial Exposition celebration in Philadelphia. The bridge cost $37 million and has been characterized as the "first distinctly modern suspension bridge built on a grand scale." It was an instant success, attracting thirty-five thousand vehicles a day to cross the Delaware at twenty-five cents a passage.

The bridge is 128 feet wide and 8,291 feet from portal to portal—9,620 feet when the plazas are included. The structure's 1,750 foot-long center span was the world's longest single suspension span for a while. Its towers rise nearly 400 feet above the river. Over twenty-five thousand miles of cable were used in two main cables, each thirty inches in diameter.

Its name was changed to the Benjamin Franklin Bridge in 1956 to mark the 250th anniversary of Franklin's birth and to distinguish it from the newly constructed Walt Whitman Bridge. The Delaware River Port Authority manages these and other spans over the Delaware, in addition to the PATCO High-Speed commuter rail line, which uses the Ben Franklin Bridge to provide service into Center City (downtown) Philadelphia.

At the water's edge was Pier 12 North, operated by the Baltimore & Ohio Railroad for general freight purposes and where the railroad docked its floating barges. Pier 12 today is home to the Philadelphia Marine Center. This is Philadelphia's leading boating facility, offering 338 deep-water slips.

The Pennsylvania Railroad used Piers 13 and 15 North as a city freight station, shipping 1,800,000 tons annually of general merchandise carried in railroad cars on car floats. About four hundred men worked at these wharves, which are no longer around. Octo Waterfront Grille is at Pier 15 today.

The Summer Street Steps

The bank stairway between Vine and Race was at Summer Street, an intermittent lane that once crossed the city. This tiny street was also one of the alleys that cut through the made-earth between Water Street and Delaware Avenue. It's still there today, providing access to both North Water Street and I-95 North from Delaware Avenue.

The Summer Street Steps lasted until 1925, when the Delaware River Bridge's Philadelphia Anchorage was completed. The stairwell was removed as part of grading and paving around the gargantuan structure. A work contract drawing showing existing conditions labels a set of "Stone Steps Down" on the line of Summer Street between Front and Water. Another drawing shows that the steps were replaced with a concrete sidewalk. That sidewalk must have lasted until the 1970s, when Interstate 95 came through.

The Philadelphia Anchorage extends from Columbus Boulevard to Front Street. Its foundations required twenty-eight thousand cubic yards of concrete and go down sixty-three feet to bedrock. The excavation yielded some surprises. The following is from the final engineering report for the bridge, issued in 1927:

> *It was known that old bulkhead walls existed between Delaware Avenue and Water Street at the site of the Philadelphia anchorage. Test pits excavated before the buildings were demolished disclosed considerable timber cribbing of this nature. Some of it had evidently served as foundations for earlier buildings, but most of it was probably wharf construction along the water front of Colonial days. Since buried timbers of any considerable size would offer a serious obstacle to dredging operations, the specifications provided that the site should be prepared by stripping so much of the overlying fill as found necessary to remove all old foundations and buried timbers. During these operations, hewn oak timbers 24 inches square and parts of a barge or boat framed with wooden pins were removed.*

Many commercial buildings were cleared to build the Philadelphia Anchorage in the early 1920s, and half of Water Street was eliminated between Race and Vine. What's more, the imposing structure's sudden appearance surely hastened the waterfront's decline. Besides interrupting Water Street, the Delaware River Bridge visibly transported people and vehicles high above and away from that part of town. The obvious psychological effect was that the riverside commercial district was unworthy.

Construction of Interstate 95 had an even more devastating physical and psychological effect five decades later.

8

Race to Arch

Fighting Fires and Rats Near America's Oldest Urban Street

Race Street was originally called Songhurst Street after John Songhurst, a friend of William Penn and an original Quaker settler of Philadelphia. Its name then became Sassafras Street.

The street's current name came about because this was the main roadway heading to horse races that occurred at or around Center Square (where Philadelphia City Hall is today) and because of occasional horse races on the street dating back to the 1720s. The designation continued long after the racing ended.

Race Street Connector and Civic Plans for Philadelphia's Waterfront

Race Street east of Second Street was shifted roughly thirty feet north during Interstate 95's construction. The altered street winds its way under the highway overpass—an unappealing tunnel for pedestrians to use in accessing the Delaware River from Center City.

To meet the long-standing need to enhance this streetscape, the Race Street Connector project of 2011 added wider sidewalks and landscaping. Plus, an LED light screen attached to the viaduct's underside displays abstract images of the river in real time, to remind pedestrians that a river lies ahead. In announcing funding from the William Penn Foundation for these improvements, Mayor Michael Nutter declared in early 2011: "We will have one of the best waterfronts in America."

The Race Street Connector is a project of the Delaware River Waterfront Corporation (DRWC). A successor to the Penn's Landing Corporation, this nonprofit corporation acts as the steward of the riverfront so as to provide a benefit to inhabitants and visitors of Philadelphia. DRWC intends to transform the seven-mile sweep of the city's river frontage between Allegheny and Oregon Avenues into a destination location for recreational, cultural and commercial activities. Race Street is the first of about a dozen streets slated to be improved with easier access to the Delaware.

RACE STREET PIER AND PIER 9 NORTH

The Race Street Connector will definitely provide and promote access to Race Street Pier. This once-abandoned municipal pier was turned into a verdant riverside park in early 2011. Its upper level provides a sky promenade and almost forty white swamp oak trees, while a lower terrace offers seating

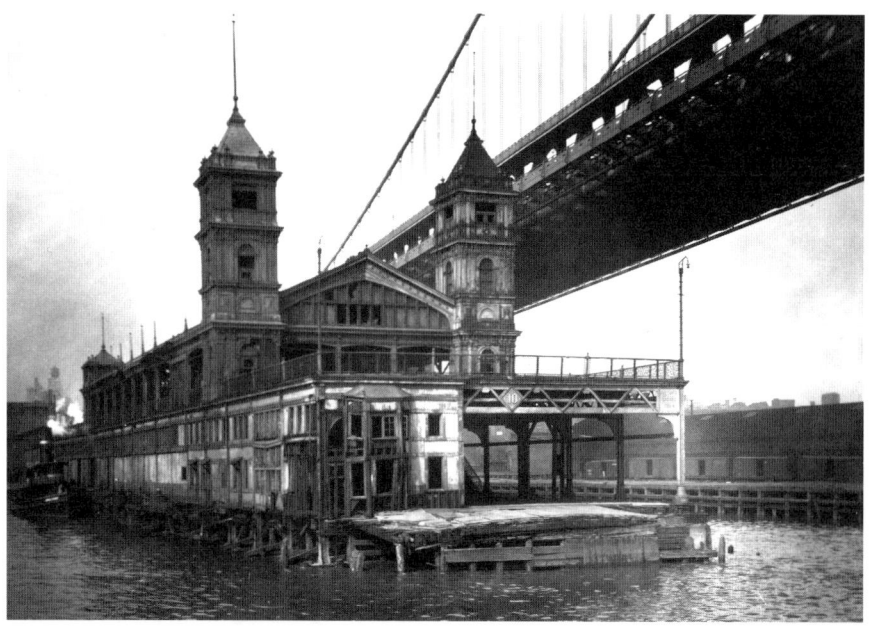

Race Street Pier was looking shabby by 1931, just before it was rebuilt and lost its recreational pavilion. *Philadelphia City Archives*.

for social activity and passive recreation. This new park on the water was the first significant public space designed and built by the DRWC. On May 12, 2011, Mayor Nutter presided over the official ceremony that placed the pier, once again, into public service. Project cost: at least $7 million.

The city constructed the pier about 1900 at a cost of $409,532. The north side was used as berths for fireboats and harbor police craft while the south side was leased for freight service, mostly tropical fruits of the United Fruit Company. At 540 feet long, Race Street Pier could accommodate most cargo ships and passenger liners of that day. It was first labeled Pier 10 and was renamed Pier 11 after being rebuilt in 1931.

The modern use of this renovated pier relates back to when it had a pavilion (with four turrets) on its upper level, covered but open at the sides. There, people would enjoy themselves by strolling and breathing fresh river air over the Delaware. Firemen would dry their firehouses inside the turret towers. The pavilion was dismantled during the 1931 rebuild. The warehouse structure was subsequently taken off the substructure, and the pier sat flat and forlorn for decades.

South of Race Street Pier is Pier 9 North, a concrete and steel structure (with a monitor roof) that was completed in 1919 for $867,000. Banana boats used to unload their cargoes at this city-owned pier. It was common to see long lines of wagons on Delaware Avenue waiting their turn to drive into this warehouse to load bananas destined for market stalls throughout Philadelphia. Despite looking old and tired, Pier 9 is sound and is used for storage. It may ultimately become a performance or exhibition venue.

Contagion by the Delaware (I of II): The Philadelphia Rat Receiving Station

The front of Race Street Pier was a place to be avoided a century ago, for the Rat Receiving Station of the Philadelphia Bureau of Health was located there. Rats were a big problem all along the Delaware, and city officials sought ways to get rid of them and the diseases they carried (bubonic plague in particular).

At least six special agents maintained scores of rat traps along the river from Girard Avenue to Reed Street. They also rat-proofed buildings on the riverfront and inspected ships docking along the Delaware. Horse-drawn wagons marked RAT PATROL aided their efforts and emphasized their authority. More than anything, the agents enforced a rule mandating

PHILADELPHIA'S LOST WATERFRONT

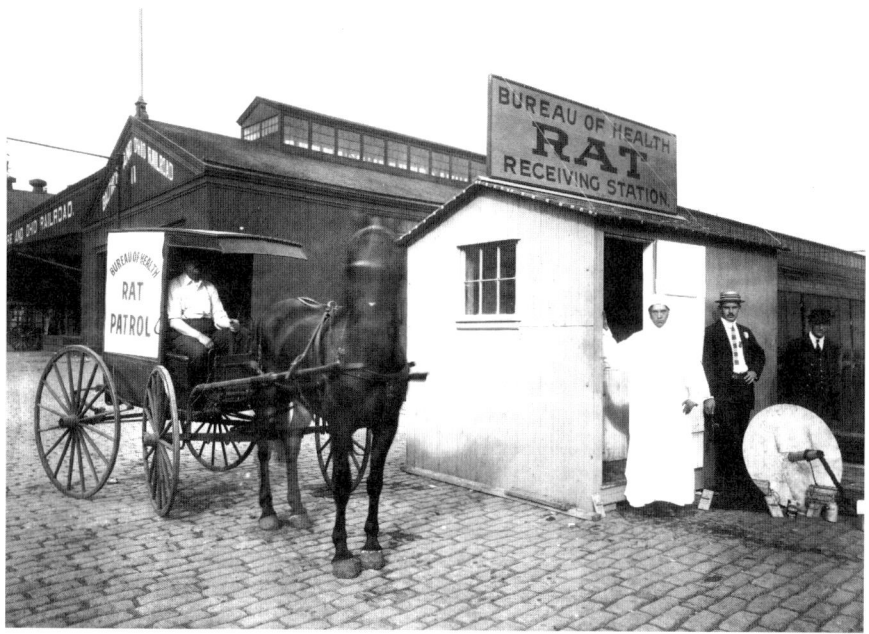

The Philadelphia Rat Receiving Station in front of Race Street Pier, along with a RAT PATROL wagon, 1914. *Philadelphia City Archives.*

that all vessels from rat-infested ports had to have rat guards on their mooring lines.

Moreover, citizens were encouraged to bring rats to the station for a bounty: five cents for live ones and two cents for dead ones. The station was established in 1914 and collected over five thousand rats by year's end.

THE HIGH PRESSURE FIRE SERVICE BUILDING

The High Pressure Fire Service (HPFS) building directly across Race Street Pier is one of the most important yet unappreciated edifices in Philadelphia. This red brick Victorian structure served the city for one hundred years, providing high-pressure water, at a moment's notice, for use in fighting fires. Along with the high-pressure pipeline system that distributed the water, this building is the main reason why Center City Philadelphia never suffered a catastrophic fire during the 1900s.

Philadelphia's regular-pressure water had become ineffective in fighting fires in increasingly larger and higher buildings in the central business

Race to Arch

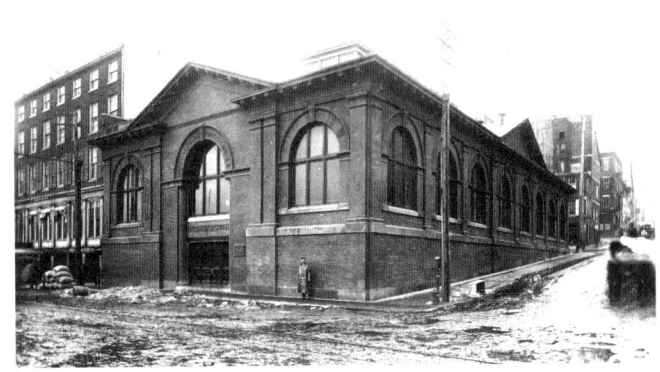

The High Pressure Fire Service building in 1904, just after completion. It looks much the same today, though a little worse for wear. *Philadelphia City Archives.*

district. Years of prodding by insurance companies and the Philadelphia Fire Department spurred the city to install the world's first high-pressure water service in a major city. Inaugurated in 1901 and completed in 1903, the system delivered water via independent pipes and special red fire hydrants located on every block between the Delaware River and Broad Street, from Race to Walnut.

The HPFS building on Delaware Avenue drew water right from the river via a twenty-inch main and supplied a network of twelve- and sixteen-inch mains. Seven 280-horsepower pumps were powered by engines operating on city gas—an early use of internal combustion engines for such work. Full pressure was available within two minutes from the time a fire alarm was sounded.

The system had the capacity of pushing ten thousand gallons of water a minute at up to three hundred pounds of pressure, with power to throw a two-inch stream 230 feet vertically. Fireboats on the Delaware were also used for backup. They connected to the system via a manifold that still protrudes from the sidewalk in front of Race Street Pier.

Fire losses immediately dropped after the HPFS system was operational, prompting the removal of extra insurance charges imposed on structures within the congested downtown. Other pumping stations followed around the city when the system was expanded into surrounding neighborhoods. The system's success brought about similar high-pressure water systems in other American cities. Philadelphia's was acknowledged as the best in the world for years and years.

The fifty-six-mile system lasted until 2005, when it was decommissioned after falling into disrepair. High-pressure water service had become unnecessary anyway due to better firefighting equipment, high-rise sprinklers and fire-

Philadelphia's Lost Waterfront

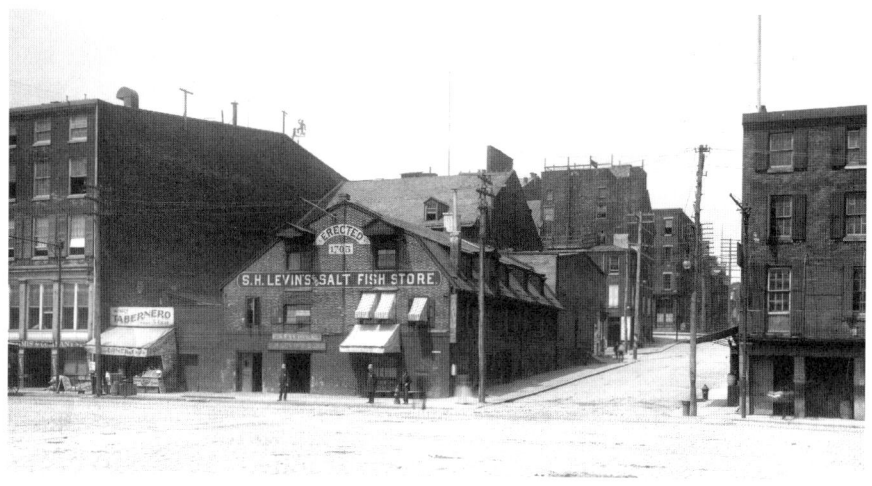

The Salt Fish Store was built in 1705 where the HPFS building is today. This undated photo shows the steepness of Race Street as it approached Delaware Avenue. Two policemen are keeping the peace. *Philadelphia City Archives.*

resistant construction materials. The HPFS building, though, still heroically stands. It is scheduled to become office and performance space for the Philadelphia Live Arts Festival (Philly Fringe). A café is also part of the scheme.

The old pumping plant sits where a salt house was situated for roughly two hundred years. This was a place to store and sell salt and salt fish. Built in 1705 with bricks and timbers imported from England, it was one of the first structures erected on this stretch of the Delaware. Other enterprises used the storehouse before it was taken down about 1903.

The Cherry Street Steps

The ten-foot-wide passageway between Race and Arch was—and still is—called Cherry Street, and the bank steps thereon were known as the Cherry Street Steps. William Penn may have directed his surveyor, Thomas Holme (1624–1695), to plan for this specific set of riverbank steps when Philadelphia was platted. (It was Holme who designed Philadelphia as a grid between the Delaware and Schuylkill Rivers.)

Since the Cherry Street Steps were adjacent to property that Holme owned on Front Street, he or his heirs may have installed the stairwell. There's evidence of this in Irma Corcoran's book *Thomas Holme, 1624–1695* (1992):

Race to Arch

Thomas Holme was to leave a cartway thirty feet along the bank... Moreover, he was to lay out his proportion and part so that in the center between Mulberry and Sassafras Streets a public thoroughfare ten feet wide could be made down from the east side of Delaware Front Street.

The Cherry Street Steps are the most documented of any of the lost Penn steps, at least in terms of illustrations and photographs. The staircase was drawn many times by Philadelphia artist Joseph Pennel. And a charming photograph taken by G. Mark Wilson shows a man and a woman in the stairwell. According to *Still Philadelphia* (1983):

Wilson's quest for picturesque Philadelphia led him to quaint scenes, some superficially evocative of Europe. He captioned this early 1920s photograph "not in Florence, Genoa or Naples," but the facts he supplied with the image make it clear that the scene was uniquely American. The couple seemed to be courting. The man, Wilson noted, was Jewish, the woman Irish, a circumstance almost unimaginable where Old-World customs and proscriptions still held sway.

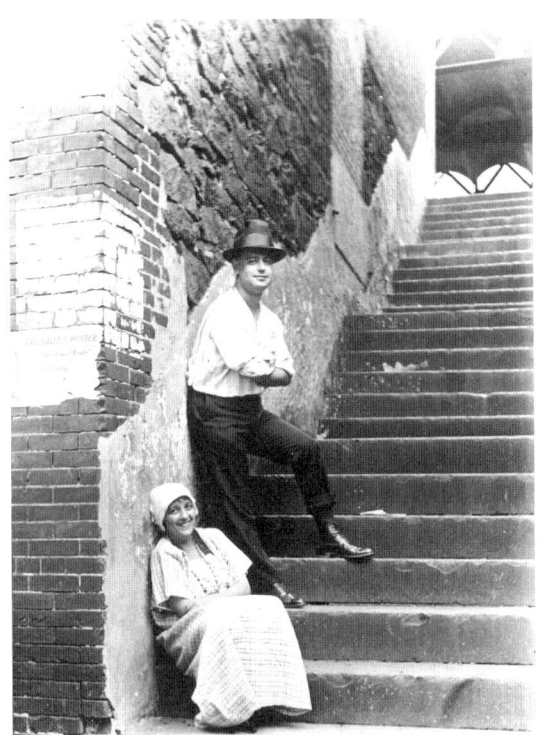

The Cherry Street Steps about 1920. Notice the Frankford El structure atop Front Street in the background. *The Library Company of Philadelphia.*

Philadelphia's Lost Waterfront

Undeniably, this was an immigrant community in the 1920s.
These bank steps were obliterated for sure when I-95 barreled through Philadelphia in the late 1960s.

Elfreth's Alley

John Watson, in his *Annals*, refers to the Cherry Street Steps as the Elfreth's Alley Steps. This is because they were a bit south of Elfreth's Alley, now a popular tourist attraction between Front and Second Streets. This National Historic Landmark District is the oldest continuously occupied residential street in the United States.

Elfreth's Alley was opened in 1702 by John Gilbert and Arthur Wells, two property owners who combined their land to create a subdivision through the city block they owned. The alleyway's namesake was Jeremiah Elfreth, a blacksmith who rented several houses on the block to sea captains, stevedores, shipwrights and craftsmen, some who worked in the same buildings where they resided. It has been the home to all sorts of people in its more than three hundred years, from wealthy friends of Benjamin Franklin to immigrant families.

During the Industrial Revolution, the alley became an enclave for European immigrants seeking new lives in North America. As such, they were not all that different than the Quaker settlers who lived in caves by the Delaware River. The tiny row homes on Elfreth's Alley are excellent examples of Philadelphia's Colonial, Georgian and

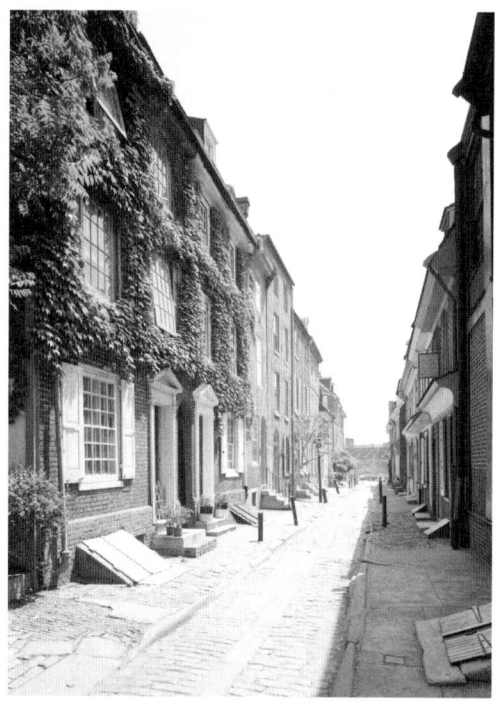

Looking east on Elfreth's Alley in 1972. Most Philadelphia alleys by the Delaware resembled this scene long ago. Many are still around. Elfreth's Alley is the best known and looks even better today. *Library of Congress (HABS)*.

Race to Arch

Federal housing of the eighteenth and nineteenth centuries. Most are private dwellings to this day.

The alley had become an impoverished neighborhood by World War I and faced possible demolition. In 1934, a group of individuals formed the Elfreth's Alley Association to save several houses from being torn down by absentee landlords. They later helped rescue the alley from other threats, including construction of I-95.

Fireman's Hall Museum is on Second Street next to the alley, housed in a 1902 firehouse. This is one of the nation's premier museums on firefighting, many advances of which were developed in Philadelphia.

The Bank Meeting House was once on the riverbank south of Elfreth's Alley. Built in 1685, this early Quaker house of worship was used for 104 years before it was pulled down. The relocated Front Street between Race and Arch runs through ground on which this brick structure stood.

SLEDDING TOWARD THE RIVER—NO MORE

Watson wrote that "[t]hirty to forty boys and sleds could be seen running down each of the streets descending from Front street to the river" in his youth. The streets had been graded by his time to better join the "upper" and "lower" planes of Penn's City. Watson's sledding comment illustrates how the embankment's natural grade between Arch and Market Streets was where the change in height was the most pronounced.

There's definitely no sledding on these streets nowadays, chiefly because Interstate 95 truncated many of the east–west streets on the Delaware's edge. Arch was one of these streets—blocked off with a solid brick wall that runs along the east side of Front. There was no way to avoid this since the superhighway changes from a below-grade to an elevated structure between Race and Market. The brusque disconnect of Arch Street from the waterfront of which it was such an integral part is truly regrettable. The same goes for Vine Street.

Other key east–west streets cut short from the river by I-95 include Market, Chestnut (excepting a motor vehicle viaduct connection to Penn's Landing and Market Street), Walnut (excepting a pedestrian overpass to Penn's Landing), Pine, Lombard, South (excepting a pedestrian walkway over the highway), Bainbridge, Fitzwater and Catherine. Not to mention Willow, Noble and Poplar Streets in Northern Liberties and numerous minor streets and alleys leading to the river all along the Delaware.

9

Arch to Market

Inventors and Millionaires by the Delaware (Enter Stephen Girard)

Arch Street was first called Holme Street, after Penn's surveyor, Thomas Holme. Then it became Mulberry Street.

Early on, this east–west lane was dug down east of Second Street to make it level with the Delaware shoreline, in order to allow for easier access to docks and ferry slips at the end of Mulberry Street. A single-span arched bridge was constructed to carry Front Street over the lowered road. Hence, Philadelphians began to refer to Mulberry as "the arch street." The stone archway was taken away in 1721 after falling into disrepair and becoming a public nuisance, as Watson notes at length in his *Annals*. But the name stuck.

The Arch Street Wharf

There were two sets of bank steps on this block, along with five alleys passing through various wharf facilities built atop made-earth east of Water Street. The northernmost set of steps between Front and Water connected to Old Ferry Alley, which led to the ferry landings on the river.

One of these was the Arch Street Wharf, constructed in 1690 and prominent in colonial times. It was here that an unclaimed shipment of coffee was left to rot in the hot humid summer of 1793, leading Dr. Benjamin Rush to conclude, incorrectly, that this was the source of Philadelphia's deadly yellow fever epidemic that year (more about this in chapter seventeen).

Arch to Market

The Arch Street Landing remained at the heart of the city's commerce on the Delaware River well into the 1800s. It was located approximately where Delaware Avenue and Highway 95 run in front of Pier 5 Condominium today.

Watson relates an amusing incident that occurred in the 1730s or so just west of the wharf/landing at what was once 87–89 Water Street: "[O]ld Anthony Wilkinson had his cabin once in this bank, which got blown up by a drunken Indian laying his pipe on some gunpowder in it." The place where this happened existed for over two centuries afterward, becoming part of Philadelphia's lore first through eyewitnesses and then through John Watson's chronicle. That spot no longer exists owing to I-95.

JOHN FITCH AND OLIVER EVANS

The era of the steamship began at the Arch Street Wharf on July 20, 1786. It was from there, on that date, that Pennsylvania-based inventor John Fitch (1743–1798) navigated the first vessel ever successfully driven by steam. The test of his small skiff on the Delaware River was the earliest practical application of steam power to navigation in the world.

The next year, Fitch made the first public demonstration of a steamboat in the presence of delegates from the Constitutional Convention, which was then in session at the Pennsylvania State House (Independence Hall). Simply named *Steam-Boat*, Fitch's cumbersome craft was forty feet long and had six

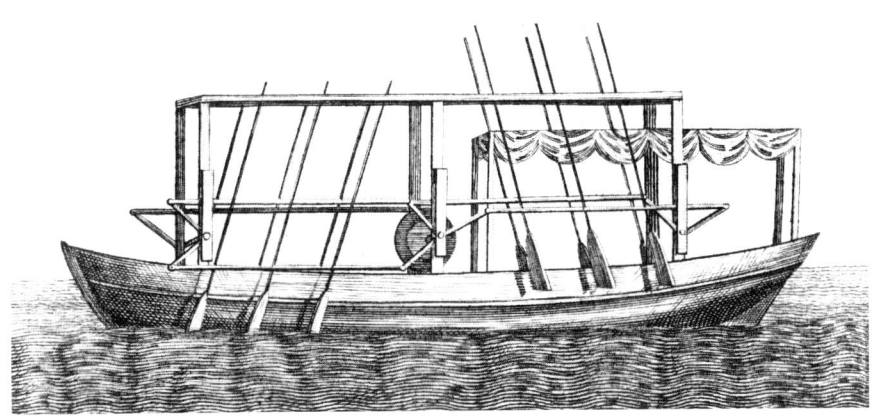

Plan of John Fitch's *Steam-Boat*. *Library of Congress.*

paddles on each side connected to a twelve-inch cylinder steam engine. It made three miles per hour against the current.

Fitch soon inaugurated a ferry business between Philadelphia and Camden, departing regularly from the Arch Street Landing. This was the world's first steam ferry service. He later began transporting passengers and freight between Philadelphia and Burlington, New Jersey, as well as points south of Philadelphia. The *Steam-Boat* cruised almost three thousand miles in 1790 alone.

In all, John Fitch constructed four steamboats that demonstrated the feasibility of using steam for water locomotion. He received a U.S. patent for his invention on August 26, 1791. Yet while his boats were mechanically sound, Fitch was not able to rouse support for his new method of ship propulsion. He never attained riches and was rewarded with only ridicule for his work. Nevertheless, Fitch was the most important of the handful of men who built steam vessels before Robert Fulton introduced his *Clermont*.

Other inventors experimented on the Delaware River with applying steam to watercraft in the late 1700s and early 1800s. Oliver Evans (1755–1819) of Philadelphia invented a steam-driven amphibious dredge that he called the *Oruktor Amphibolos* (amphibious digger). In 1805, Evans floated it down the Schuylkill River, steamed it up the Delaware to the central waterfront and then drove it west on Market Street back to where he started.

The contraption was intended to clear away river mud that constantly accumulated between the city's docks, but it turned out to be inefficient for that purpose. Still, this was the first motorized vehicle in America and the world's second motorized carriage, as well as the first steam-powered land vehicle in the world. General Motors once credited the *Oruktor Amphibolos* as the forerunner of the modern automobile. It was also a distant ancestor of today's Ride the Ducks amphibious vehicles that take tourists around Philadelphia and then plunge into the Delaware for a cruise on the river.

Patent No. 1 and Five-Pointed Stars

Samuel Hopkins (1765–1840) was another local inventor associated with Arch Street near the Delaware. This Philadelphia Quaker was granted the very first patent under the Patent Act of the United States on July 31, 1790. Hopkins lived on the north side of Arch between Front and Second Streets.

Signed by President Washington and Secretary of State Jefferson, United States Patent No. 1 was for an improvement "in the making of Pot ash and

Pearl ash by a new Apparatus and Process." Hopkins's patent was noteworthy not only because it was the first of its kind but also because it was vitally linked to the fledgling nation's economy. Potash, America's first industrial chemical, is an impure form of potassium carbonate.

One block farther west on Arch Street is the Betsy Ross House, the supposed home of another inventive person. Betsy Ross's role in sewing the nation's first flag is subject to dispute, but the skilled upholsterer most certainly contributed to the Stars and Stripes's design by changing its stars from six to five points—five-pointed stars were easier to cut from cloth. At the very least, Ross represents the many artisan women of Philadelphia who ran businesses and supported their families during the colonial and federal periods.

Filbert Street Steps (Tresse's Stairs) and Clifford's Alley

The steps and lower alley of Old Ferry Alley must have been abandoned in the mid-1800s, as Abraham Ritter notes: "Passing a flight of steps to Water street (now closed), a little below, at No. 53 [North Front]."

The southernmost stepped alleyway on that block was located at 29 North Water. Initially called Tresse's Stairs, the stairway was installed by Thomas Tresse, a notable merchant with scores of mercantile enterprises in Philadelphia's early days.

These stairs and the alley leading to the river were later named Clifford's Alley, since they led to Clifford's Wharf on the Delaware. Ships left for Boston, Savannah and other coastal ports from this place. The alley and wharf were named after Thomas Clifford, whose business was at 29 North Water Street. He and his family were shipowners and importers of hardware from Liverpool.

A corner of Clifford's dock had collapsed into the Delaware in the early nineteenth century. Nicknamed "the broken wharf," it became a convenient place for boys to go swimming. This was an early leisure activity done amid Philadelphia's busy working waterfront.

Stephen Girard (and His Townhouse)

Bordering Clifford's Wharf were the wharves of sailor, shipping magnate and banker Stephen Girard (1750–1831). Other Girard properties surrounded his docks, including his home and attached office (i.e., "counting house") at 23 North Water Street and his warehouse at 31 and/or 33 North Water Street. Girard was previously at 43 North Front, as Ritter records:

> *In 1791, and long before, No. 43* [North Front], *at the south corner of another flight of steps to Water street, our late opulent Stephen Girard, was proprietor of a greengrocery, where edibles to all tastes, from an onion to an apple and a bean to a slice of pork, could be had for the money. He occupied through to Water street, and could sell at No. 31 there as at No. 43 above.*

Stephen Girard resided at his Water Street town house overlooking the Delaware River for almost forty years. He lived with several young housekeepers, perhaps some of whom were mistresses, after he committed his wife to Pennsylvania Hospital in 1790. The daughter of a Philadelphia shipbuilder, Mary Lum (1758–1815) had suffered a debilitating mental illness after several years of marriage, causing her to be prone to emotional outbursts and fits of violence. She spent the rest of her life in the hospital's insanity ward. The situation caused Girard great sadness, since he professed to love her and especially since he never had an heir.

As a result, the French émigré focused his efforts on working and making money. At his house, he managed his investments and land acquisitions to accumulate a vast fortune. Here, he devised ways to use his money and personal credit to finance the War of 1812 for the United States. He entertained Talleyrand, Louis Philippe, Joseph Bonaparte (Napoleon's brother and ex-king of Spain and Naples) and many distinguished French diplomats and refugees.

Girard and his servants could gaze south from the tall mansion's windows and rooftop balcony, searching for his cargo-laden vessels as they made their way up the Delaware from around the world to dock at his wharves. He owned some eighteen ships, and his packets—ships that sailed on a regular schedule—were the foremost line afloat at that time.

Girard spent much time at his mahogany desk, drinking imported wine and orchestrating his various commercial activities or reading the works of Voltaire, Diderot and Rousseau. He also contemplated ways to bequeath his money, including the founding of a school for "poor, white, male orphans," and ways to improve his adopted city of Philadelphia.

Girard grew old and lonely at his waterside home, with only the wants of his business dealings to keep him occupied. Here, he passed away at age eighty-one the day after Christmas 1831, the richest man in America—his

Arch to Market

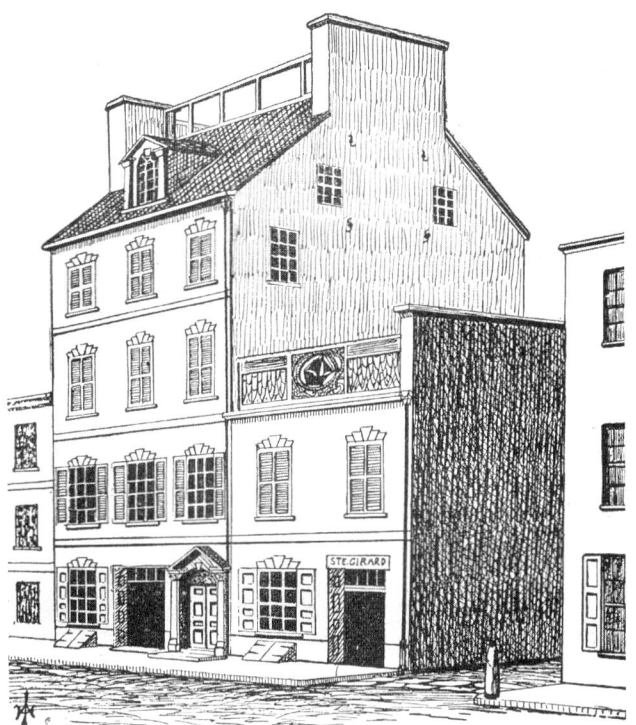

Right: Drawing of Stephen Girard's house on Water Street. *From* The Life and Character of Stephen Girard of the City of Philadelphia *(1886)*.

Below: Site of Stephen Girard's house today. The Philadelphia Anchorage of the Benjamin Franklin Bridge is in the background. *Photo by the author.*

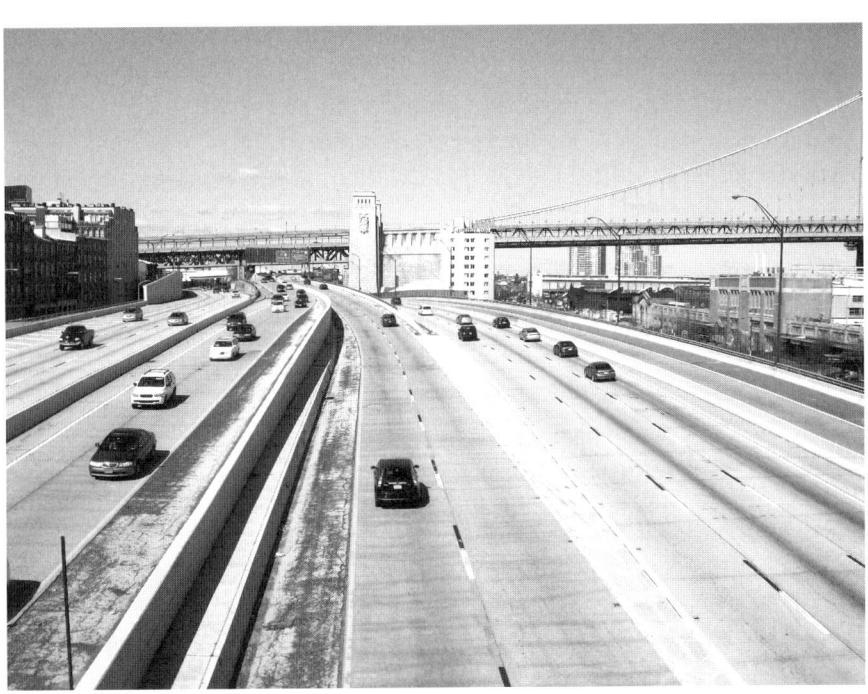

estate was about $7.5 million. And here, his infamous thirty-five-page will was read for the first time to his relations and others while his body lay in repose in the parlor.

The four-story house stood until the 1840s, when it was torn down and replaced with stores. The Delaware Expressway now covers the site completely. But incredibly, all of Stephen Girard's household possessions still exist. These items—furniture, paintings, silver and textiles made in Philadelphia, England, France and China—are on display inside Founder's Hall at Girard College.

Nathan Trotter and Frank Winne

Another importer/exporter who did very well in Philadelphia's river district was Nathan Trotter (1787–1853), born on Elfreth's Alley into a Quaker household. He lived and worked in this part of town all his life, plying his trade as a metals refiner and broker. Trotter grew rich and, like Girard, died a millionaire.

His firm, Nathan Trotter & Company, was headquartered at 36 North Front Street for over 150 years. His storehouse remains standing and is now a condominium. Still in business in Coatesville, Pennsylvania, Nathan Trotter & Co. is the oldest metals manufacturer and distributor in the United States.

That both Trotter and Girard became so moneyed while living a mere block from each other along the Delaware is remarkable. Other millionaires lived and labored on the Philadelphia waterfront; they will be profiled in subsequent chapters.

The one-time offices and warehouse of Frank W. Winne & Son are next to Trotter's building. Founded in Philadelphia in 1895, Winne was the nation's largest maker, importer and distributor of ropes, twines and packaging products—all in high demand during Philadelphia's bygone mercantile period. The Winne buildings are now apartments, and the Winne company is still based in the Philadelphia area.

This block of Front Street most epitomizes the thoroughfare at the peak of its commercial and maritime importance—at least the west side of the block. The east side has disappeared as a result of I-95. And, of course, comparable four- and five-story structures that once flanked both Water Street and Delaware Avenue are gone due to the highway.

Arch to Market

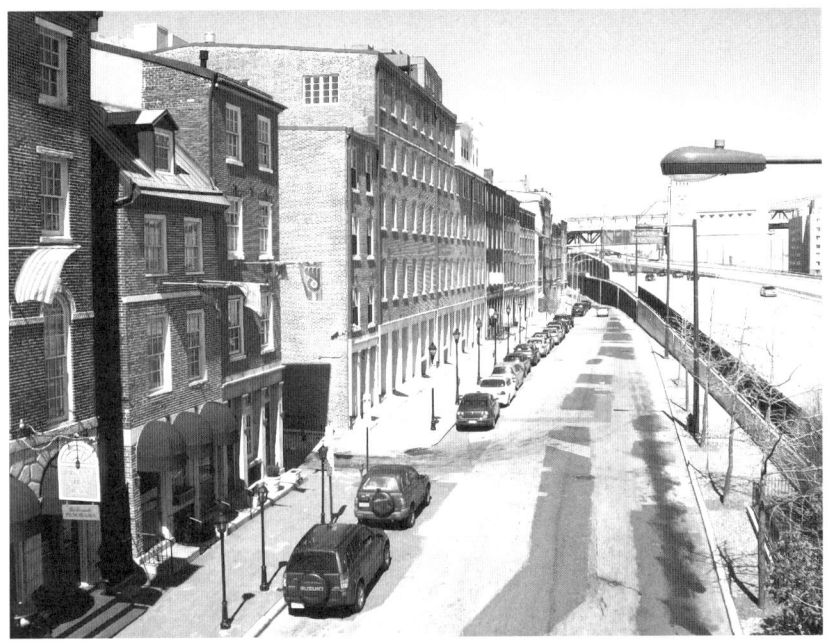

Front Street today, showing Penn's View Hotel/Ristorante Panorama, Old City Mercantile (Girard's Warehouses) and the Nathan Trotter and Frank Winne buildings. All structures are from the early to mid-1800s. Note how I-95 cuts off Front Street. *Photo by the author.*

STEPHEN GIRARD'S WILL (I OF III)

Stephen Girard left the City of Philadelphia some $500,000—an immense sum in the 1830s—for use in improving the riverfront area east of Front Street. Almost the whole rise in importance of the Port of Philadelphia is traceable to this bequest.

Girard was obviously well acquainted with Penn's stairways, given that he lived among them and one abutted his home. In his will, after explaining his understanding of how the bank steps and alleys came to be public property, Girard expressed dismay that some were no longer accessible:

> [O]*wing to neglect or to some other cause on the part of those who have had the care of the city property, several encroachments have been made on them by individuals, by wholly occupying, or building over them, or otherwise.*

This was a time when both rich and poor lived alongside one another, a common occurrence in Philadelphia until the end of the 1800s. So it's not surprising that Girard was concerned about the detrimental effect this was having on the health of people who lived on the crammed riverbank: "[I]n that way, the inhabitants, more particularly those who reside in the neighbourhood, are deprived of the benefit of that wholesome air, which [the alleys'] opening and cleansing throughout would afford."

Some modern accounts have it that the bank steps were built under the terms of Girard's will, but this is not the case. Later chapters will address the will further.

OLD CITY MERCANTILE/PENN'S VIEW HOTEL/ RISTORANTE PANORAMA

Delaware Avenue in front of Pier 3 Condominium occupies the space where Stephen Girard's docks and wharves were located long ago.

Some of his warehouses still stand on the west side of Front Street (20–30 North Front) and have been converted into residential apartments. Called the Old City Mercantile, this development is a splendid restoration of a group of Greek Revival–style buildings that had been on the brink of collapse for years. They were originally constructed between 1828 and 1834 by Girard and his estate.

Penn's View Hotel is next on Front Street on the south side of Church Street. This boutique hotel is home to Ristorante Panorama, an eatery serving fine Italian cuisine. Wine lovers around the globe have heard about its cruvinet, the world's largest wine preservation and dispensing system.

The structure that makes up the Penn's View Hotel was built as a shipping warehouse in 1828. It became a hardware store around the turn of the twentieth century and then a coffeehouse in the 1950s. The building sat vacant until chef Carlo C. Sena (1922–2011) bought and refurbished it as a hotel in 1989. Penn's View is now on the National Register of Historic Places.

Sena had previously opened La Famiglia Ristorante at 8 South Front in 1976. This was a daring undertaking since Old City Philadelphia had not yet become a dining destination. The restaurateur arrived in Philadelphia as an Italian immigrant only nine years before. Carlo Sena found success only a few doors away from where Frenchman Stephen Girard and Quaker Nathan Trotter had found theirs.

Other dining venues along Front Street include: Swanky Bubbles at 14 South Front; Spasso Italian Grill a few doors south; Downey's at Front and South since 1976; Catahoula Bar & Restaurant at 775 South Front; and the

Arch to Market

dozens of other places in Old City, Society Hill and Queen Village. Parking, the scourge of the modern city, took down many old commercial buildings to allow for convenient access to these establishments.

THE DELAWARE AVENUE ELEVATED (THE FERRY BRANCH)

Clifford's Alley was later called Filbert Street, and the Filbert Street Steps were apparently at 37 North Water. They were removed in 1907–08 by the Philadelphia Rapid Transit Company (PRTC) for the building of the Market Street Subway. The following is from a PRTC report issued in 1908:

> *Filbert Street, an 8 foot passageway for pedestrians, was closed by authority of Councils and made the site of the abutment at the south end of the concrete viaduct. Front Street is so much higher than Water Street that the second stories of the properties facing on Water Street formed the cellars on the Front Street side.*

The "8 foot passageway" was the Penn stairwell at Filbert Street.

The Market Street Subway turned north at Front Street and exited the ground at a transition portal—between the subway and elevated portions—just north of Market Street. The shed covering this portal was used as a freight station for the PRTC's trolleys, which ran on both Market and Front Streets. The Front and Market Station was a lively spot in the days when freight trolleys delivered milk, newspapers, packages and other time-critical items.

The Market Street Line continued up an incline to an elevated steel structure and then turned 180 degrees in hairpin fashion above Arch Street to reach Delaware Avenue. It then proceeded over the boulevard's southbound lanes all the way to South Street, where the line stub-ended. This was the Delaware Avenue Elevated, also known as the "Ferry Branch" or "Ferry Line," since its stations served the many ferries to New Jersey. There were two stops: one at Market-Chestnut and another at South Street.

The Ferry Line lost passengers as ferry traffic diminished after the Delaware River Bridge opened in 1926. Most ferries had ceased operating by 1938, and the Ferry Branch stopped running the following year. The elevated structure atop Delaware Avenue was then dismantled. Not a single trace remains.

The Delaware Avenue El alternated service to Sixty-ninth Street with the Frankford Elevated Line, which connected to the Market Street Subway at

PHILADELPHIA'S LOST WATERFRONT

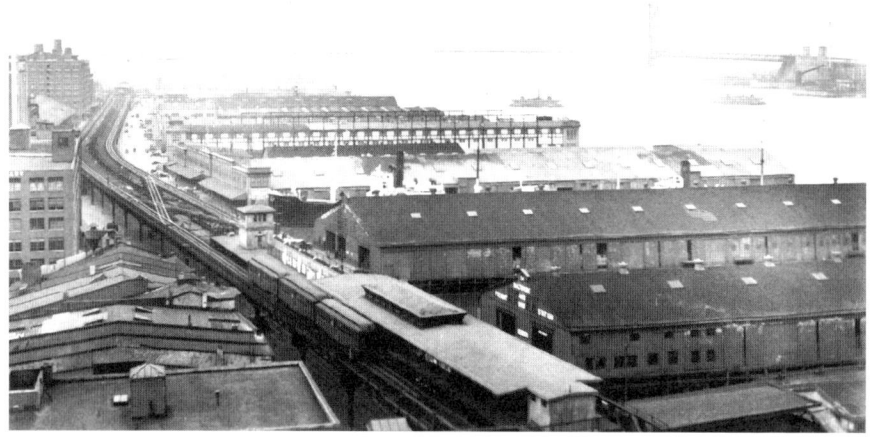

A view of the waterfront looking north about 1930, showing the Delaware Avenue Elevated atop Delaware Avenue, the El's terminus at South Street, the density of finger piers along the river and the Ben Franklin Bridge. *Philadelphia City Archives*.

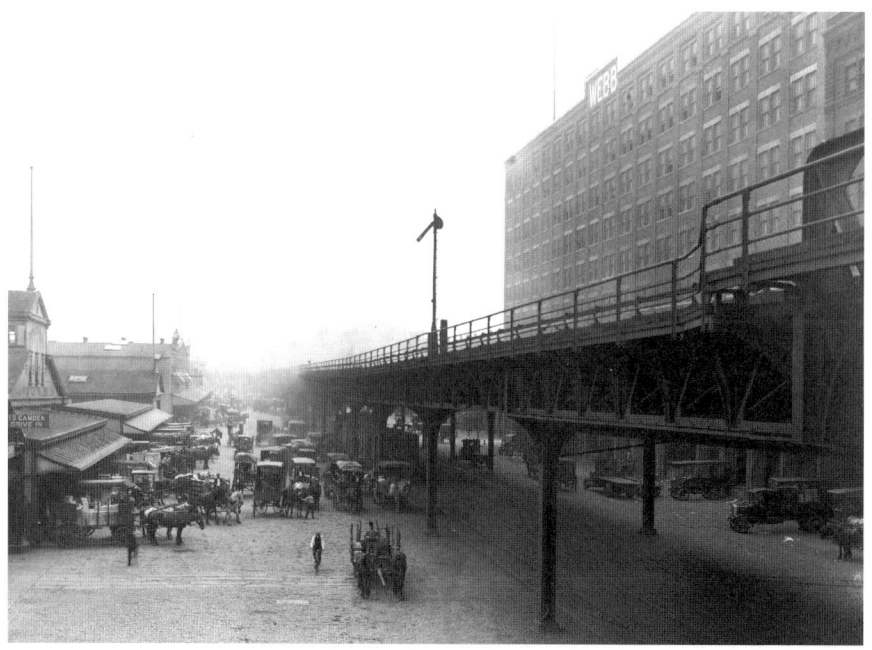

The Delaware Avenue Elevated, looking south from Chestnut Street. *Philadelphia City Archives*.

Arch to Market

Arch Street. Built by the city between 1915 and 1922, the Frankford Line ran north atop Front Street toward Philadelphia's Frankford section—and still does so.

Construction of Interstate 95 forced the removal of the transition portal on Water Street. The portal's site—once the location of the Filbert Street Steps—was then covered by the freeway. Furthermore, the Frankford El's overhead structure on Front Street was removed for over a mile north of Arch Street in the mid-1970s. (This stretch of Front had not seen the light of day in half a century.) The route of the Market-Frankford line was relocated to within the median of I-95 during the highway's construction.

PIER 3 NORTH AND PIER 5 NORTH (THE NEW GIRARD GROUP PIERS)

The Department of Wharves, Docks and Ferries built Piers 3 and 5 North in 1922 and 1923 as the last element of a fifteen-year phase of improvements to the Port of Philadelphia. These warehouse piers were specifically designed to: 1) handle ships with much greater draw, 2) enable the loading and unloading of more than one ship simultaneously and 3) facilitate the rapid transfer of cargo to railroads, wagons and trucks. The city spent $4.5 million to construct these sister piers.

Piers 3 and 5 were raised on the site of several obsolete wooden wharves that were put up in the late nineteenth century with money left to the city by Stephen Girard. These old piers were dubbed the "Girard Group" (or "Girard Piers"), so the replacement structures were officially called the New Girard Group Piers. Completed first, Pier 3 was officially dedicated by Mayor J. Hampton Moore on June 29, 1922.

The Clyde Steamship Company, which provided passenger and freight service between New York and southern ports, operated both the old and the new piers. Philadelphia was a port of call for the Clyde Lines for years and years.

The New Girard Piers were made of steel and concrete with brick and limestone facing and stand on timbers driven into the riverbed; some eight thousand poles support Pier 3 alone. Both structures extend about 550 feet into the Delaware River channel, which is as far as federal law allows to ensure safe navigation. (Being a navigable interstate river, the Delaware falls under federal jurisdiction.)

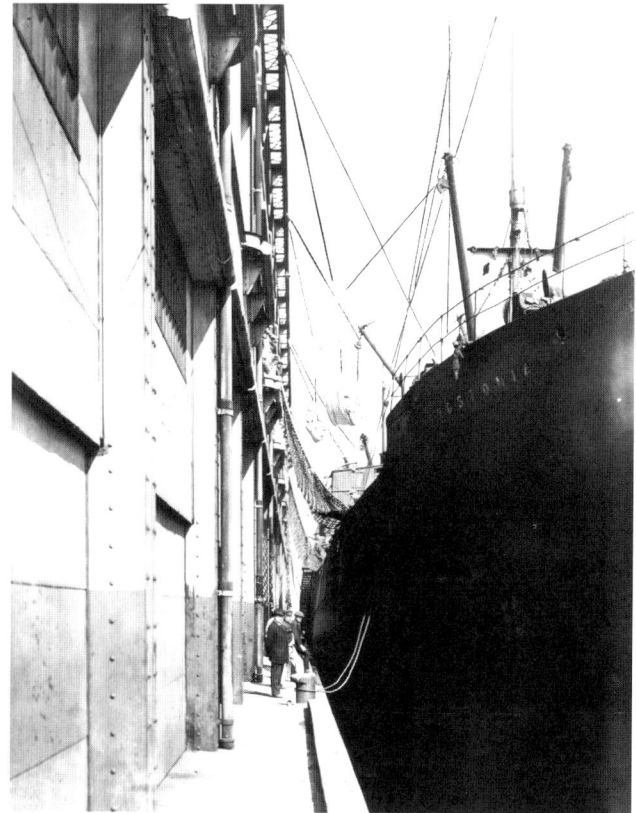

This is how cargo was transferred between ships and docks in the old days. *Philadelphia City Archives.*

Municipal Piers 3 and 5 came about right at the zenith of the central Delaware River corridor's role in Philadelphia's maritime activity, a period when the slogan "Ship Via Philadelphia" was a city mantra. The Great Depression diminished port operations considerably, although things picked up during World War II. But that was the last hurrah for this portion of the Delaware as a shipping center.

After decades of faithful service, Piers 3 and 5 North succumbed to more modern methods of port operations and cargo handling. They lingered on into the 1970s, after which they stood forsaken and neglected—and rat infested—squarely in the area that was then being transformed into Penn's Landing.

In a stroke of genius and a leap of faith, a group of developers began converting the two outmoded warehouse piers into residences beginning in 1985. While plans were drawn, the now old New Girard Group piers were added to the National Register of Historic Places in recognition of their

Arch to Market

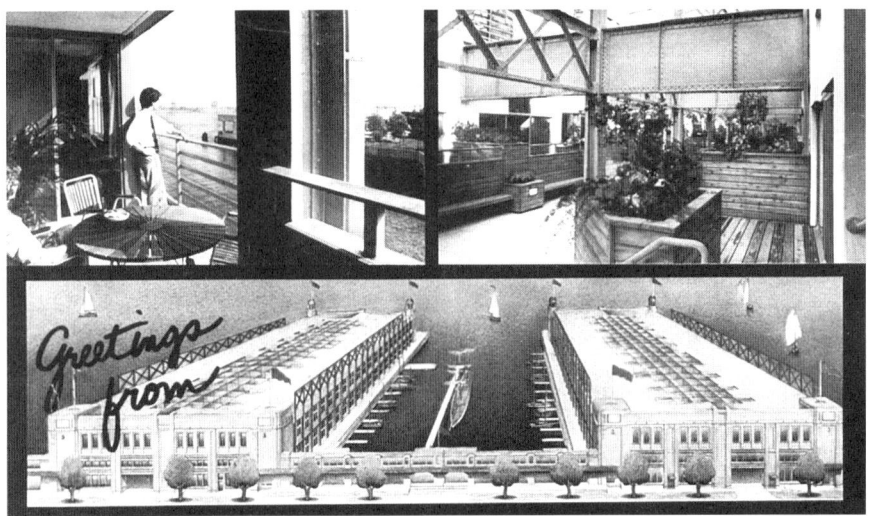

A postcard of the Piers at Penn's Landing. *Author's collection.*

early Art Deco architecture. A component of the adaptive reuse project was removing the roof of both buildings to create a tree-filled atrium in each complex. The ground floor of each structure, where rail cars used to enter, is now parking.

Pier 3 was meant to be a condominium when the rehabilitation was planned, but the housing market collapsed and the building became an apartment house in 1986. Seven years later, a Miami developer bought the place from a foreclosing bank for $8 million. The 172 units at Pier 3 were turned into condos priced from $49,000 to $139,900. They sold out within three weeks in 1994. Meanwhile, after a similar story at Pier 5, 40 of 96 units ranging from $139,900 to $289,900 sold on a single weekend.

The notion of living by the Delaware River in Philadelphia had evidently become appealing by the 1990s. Nowadays, the Piers at Penn's Landing are successful condominium complexes. A few hardy souls even live year-round on boats at the marina between the two piers.

10

At Market (High) Street

Ben Franklin, King Tamanend and Christ Church in Old City Philadelphia

Market Street is the east–west counterpart to Philadelphia's north–south Broad Street. The one-hundred-foot-wide avenue was originally named High Street, a term derived from one or both of the following: 1) "High" was the familiar name of the main street in most English towns, a custom dating back to Roman times; and 2) the street began at the highest point of the bluff that ran alongside the Delaware River when Philadelphia was founded. Writer Joseph Jackson confirms this in *Market Street, Philadelphia: The Most Historic Highway in America* (1918).

High/Market Street divided the Delaware waterfront into north and south. Piers and wharves were designated North and South depending on what side of the street they were on. Plus, for the longest time, the riverfront was characterized as being either the "North Wharves" or the "South Wharves."

The London Coffee House

Front and High was Philadelphia's first town center. The legendary London Coffee House, built in 1702, used to be on the southwest corner. Its position on Front Street (the Kingshighway) made the tavern a convenient stop for stagecoaches arriving from points north and south. The same goes for its proximity to the Delaware River. The London Coffee House became the

At Market (High) Street

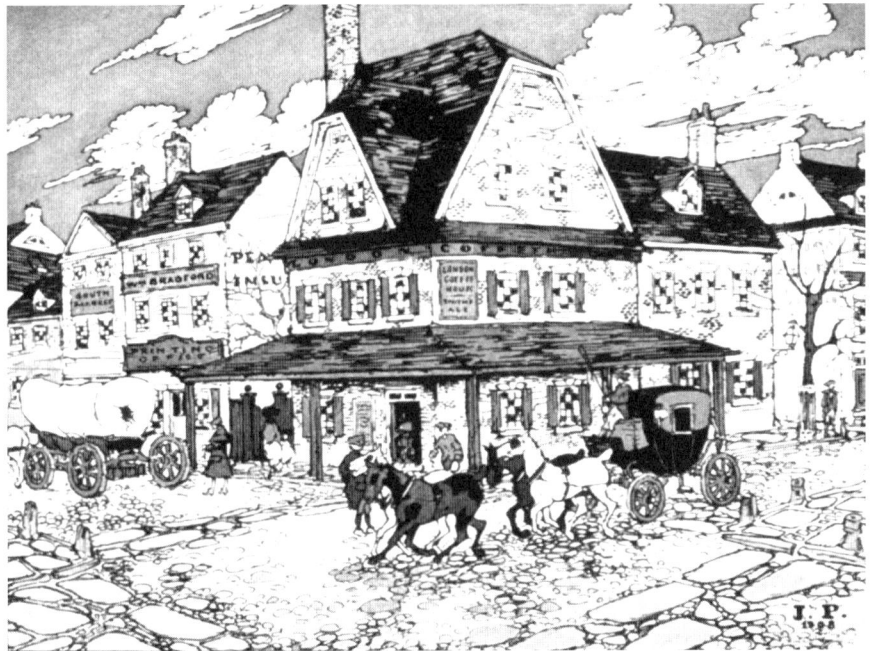

The London Coffee House at the southwest corner of Front and Market. *Library of Congress.*

most popular place in the city for both local and visiting members of the business and maritime communities to conduct business and discuss politics.

The "Widow Roberts" ran the tavern for years, serving coffee, alcoholic beverages and simple meals. When she retired in 1754, printer/publisher William Bradford took over and turned it into the first stock exchange in America.

Over pots of piping hot coffee, owners of recently arrived schooners advertised their goods, investors bought and sold real estate, fishermen boasted about their latest catch, printers gathered the news, and public auctioneers sold a variety of merchandise—as well as slaves. Revolutionary War pamphleteer Thomas Paine, boarding next door, was offended by the view of slave auctions from his window.

Philadelphia's businessmen informally established the Philadelphia Stock Exchange at the London Coffee House in 1790—preceding the New York Stock Exchange by two years. Seeing the need for more substantial accommodations, they soon moved to City Tavern (aka Merchants' Coffee House) a few blocks away.

The London Coffee House became a general store in 1791 and then a tobacco shop and cigar manufactory. It gave way in 1883 to the five-story edifice that still stands at 100 Market Street. This building was later home to the Franklin Trust Company. As of 2011, it has been vacant for some thirty years, having last been a bar and grill.

The High Street Wharf and Ben Franklin

The High Street Wharf was a bustling place early in the eighteenth century. This was where boats from Burlington came to the city, offering eighteenth-century travelers from upper New Jersey and points north the last part of their journey to Philadelphia.

One such traveler was Benjamin Franklin, who entered the city for the first time on October 6, 1723, as a dirty, tired and hungry runaway. He had come to Philadelphia, together with others, via a rowboat he helped paddle from Burlington. After leaving the wharf, he went straight to a bakery on High Street and purchased three cents' worth of bread, which turned out to be three large loaves, as the story goes.

The High Street Market Sheds

The High Street Wharf was also the main landing for boats that delivered produce grown in New Jersey. This went on for some two hundred years.

High Street began to be called Market Street about 1800 because this was where Philadelphia's first food market was based. Covered stalls were situated in the middle of the road starting at Front Street and gradually extended westward beyond Eighth Street. A crowded fish market occupied the middle of the street from Front Street to the Delaware River for decades.

The High Street Market Sheds came to rival the marketplaces of London and Paris. Farmers from the hinterlands of Philadelphia County would come into town on Wednesdays and Saturdays with their wagons of crops and meat. There, they joined farmers from the Garden State at what was sometimes called the "Jersey Market." Monetary face-offs would occur at noon on market days when rivals tried to outbid one another during horse auctions.

What is often left out of history books is that the sheds of High/Market Street served as hunting grounds for the city's many prostitutes, who would prey on the naïve rural farmers who regularly came into Philadelphia to sell their harvests.

At Market (High) Street

Indeed, the busiest precinct for streetwalkers was the city's waterfront in the eighteenth century and afterward. Dozens of ships docked at Philadelphia's wharves every day, filled with seafarers who had not seen a woman in weeks. The ladies—often the wives or widows of sailors—took their johns back to rented rooms at sordid inns along the alleys or courtyards near the docks.

Market Street's name was made official by an ordinance of 1858—ironically, just a year before the archaic food stalls were ordered removed. All the market sheds were taken down about 1860. The bus shelter now at Front and Market was designed to look like a market stall.

The Lenni-Lenape and William Penn (I of II): Chief Tamanend and His Statue

Across from the bus shelter stands an arresting statue of Chief Tamanend (ca. 1628–ca. 1698), the principal Lenni-Lenape leader who welcomed William Penn upon his arrival to this region in 1682.

Tamanend ("the Affable One") partnered with Penn ("Mikwon") to bring about the bold accord in which Quaker settlers and local Native Americans would live together in peace. The chief consequently became a folk hero identified throughout the colonies as the "patron saint of America." Beginning in Philadelphia, his memory was observed with festivals, and social groups known as the Sons of Saint Tammany sprang up during the War for Independence in opposition to the British-oriented societies of Saints George, Andrew and David. Tamanend was even nicknamed "King Tammany" as an insult to King George.

Crafted by artist Raymond Sandoval and dedicated in 1995, the *Tamanend Statue* was one of the first sculptures of a Native American in the United States. The chief stands on a turtle (representing Mother Earth) with an eagle (a messenger of the Great Spirit) on his shoulder. The eagle is grasping a wampum belt symbolizing the world-renowned "Treaty of Amity and Friendship" (discussed in chapter thirteen) between William Penn and Tamanend and his Indian colleagues.

The belt reads what Chief Tamanend reportedly announced during the 1683 treaty summit: that the Lenni-Lenape and the English colonists would "live in peace as long as the waters run in the rivers and creeks and as long as the stars and moon endure."

There's talk of moving the statue to Penn Treaty Park, where the memorable convention took place. The park is covered in a later chapter.

Ridgway House Hotel and Other Delaware Avenue Hostelries

The Ridgway House Hotel was once located at 1 Market Street, on the street's north side at Delaware Avenue. This lodge catered to visiting mariners, produce sellers and others who needed or wanted to be close to the commercial activity by the Delaware. The cheapest accommodations, for twenty-five cents a night, offered a common room with twelve beds.

The six-story building opened in 1838, about the time that Delaware Avenue was first laid out along the river. The owner was Jacob Ridgway, who also owned the Arch Street House at the foot of Arch Street.

An October 1897 newspaper article reported the suicide of a respected lawyer from West Chester, Pennsylvania, at the Ridgway House. R. Jones Monaghan was found in his room with the end of a rubber hose in his mouth and the room's gas "flowing full head." No other details were given other than that his "occasional attacks of insanity have of late years made him the object of much publicity." The attorney's eccentric behavior had been reported over the years as widely as in the *New York Times*.

The Ridgway was demolished in the 1930s, soon after the discontinuation of most ferry service between Philadelphia and Camden. A highway now passes where Mr. Monaghan took his life. The true ignominy of this situation, though, is that Market Street—the "most historic highway in America"—no longer reaches Delaware Avenue or the Delaware River as it did for some 290 years.

Modern hotels on Delaware Avenue—the Hyatt Regency at Penn's Landing and the Comfort Inn Downtown—are two blocks away in either direction from the old Ridgway House site. Interestingly, all three of these imposing edifices were built on made-earth.

The 350-room Hyatt opened in 2000, although residents of Society Hill Towers tried to stop its construction because the twenty-two-story tower would block their view of the Delaware. (Another instance of conflict about who gets to use or enjoy the river!) The ten-story Comfort Inn hotel was built in 1987 on the site of a row of decrepit commercial structures that had narrowly missed being demolished for I-95 a few years before.

Second and High Streets

The intersection of Second and High Streets was the next town center of Philadelphia. A Quaker meetinghouse surrounded by a brick wall stood at the southwest corner. This was the Great Meeting House, built in 1695 and

At Market (High) Street

enlarged in 1755. Upon arriving in Philadelphia on a Sunday morning in 1723, Benjamin Franklin made his way to this place of worship to take in a fiery sermon (as per his experience in Boston). Not hearing anything at the silent Quaker meeting, he promptly fell asleep. A restaurant-nightclub and a food store occupy that spot today.

The Continental restaurant-martini bar is on the southeast corner. This hip place was a trailblazer in Old City's renaissance when Stephen Starr opened it in 1995. Its early success catalyzed the area, and other bars and restaurants soon followed. Today, Starr Restaurants is among the fastest growing multi-concept restaurant companies in the country.

The Old Court House (aka Town Hall) stood in the precise middle of High Street above Second. Built about 1707, the building served as Philadelphia's first city hall, prison, auction house and legislative hall. It was torn down in 1837, by which time the city's municipal work had been conducted at the Pennsylvania State House for decades.

It was at Second and High Streets that Stephen Girard was struck and knocked down by a horse-drawn wagon on December 21, 1830. The wheel grazed his head, causing a gash on his face and practically cutting off his right ear. Girard was then eighty years old, and his bleeding was severe. But he refused help. Retaining his composure, he got up on his own and made his way unaided to his home on Water Street. "I am an old sailor… I can endure suffering," he said as doctors cleaned his wounds. Girard died a little over a year after the accident.

Christ Church Steeple

Anglicans of the Church of England in 1695 founded Christ Church just north of this still-busy intersection. They set up a small wooden place of worship on Second Street. They later decided to replace this with the most sumptuous church in the colonies. Constructed between 1727 and 1744, Christ Church is considered among the nation's most beautiful eighteenth-century structures, a superb example of Georgian architecture and a monument to colonial craftsmanship.

Christ Church steeple was financed first by subscription and then by two lotteries managed by Benjamin Franklin and other leading Philadelphians. The slim white tower was built by Robert Smith and was finished in 1755, when bells from Great Britain were installed. It pierced the sky at 196 feet high and was the tallest structure in North America for almost one hundred

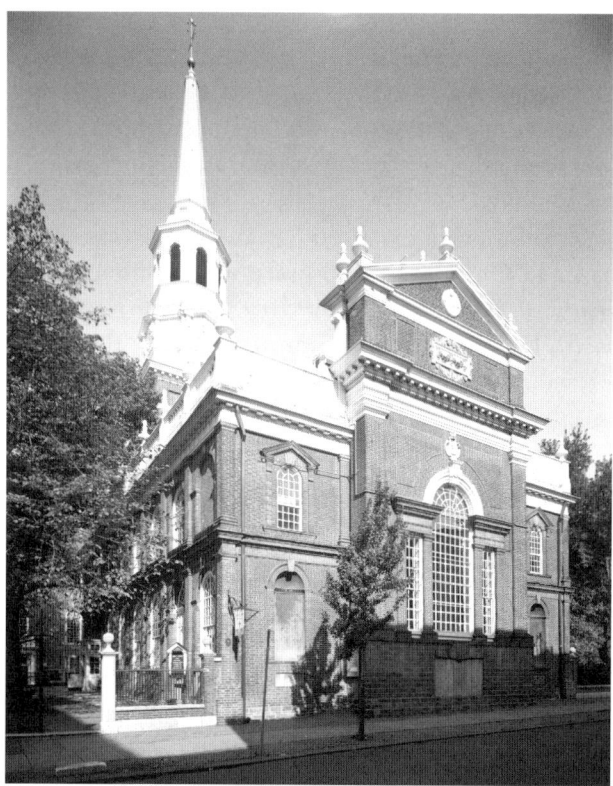

Christ Church and its steeple in 1939. The church looks the same today. *Library of Congress (HABS).*

years. John Adams wrote in his diary of climbing the tower's ladders to gaze upon the new nation in 1776.

The "Philadelphia Steeple," as it was commonly called, could be seen from miles away by seafarers sailing up the Delaware toward Philadelphia and was a beacon that guided ship captains. Even now, Christ Church steeple is a prominent landmark on the Philadelphia skyline.

Christ Church could no longer be an Anglican church due to the American Revolution. An agreement was reached between English officials of church and state and the U.S. Congress and American Anglicans to establish the Episcopal Church in America. As a result, this church is the birthplace of the Episcopal Church in the United States.

The baptismal font at Christ Church is the very one in which William Penn was baptized in 1644. It was sent to Philadelphia in 1697 from All Hallow's Church in London.

At Market (High) Street

OLD CITY PHILADELPHIA

Second and Market is still the heart of Old City Philadelphia, one of the most historic neighborhoods in the United States. Besides being among the first areas settled by Europeans in the mid-1600s and later the core of William Penn's town on the Delaware, this was undoubtedly the nation's first great crucible of commerce, finance, culture, religion and government.

The original part of Philadelphia became a temporary home to the new federal government in the eighteenth century, as well as the home and workplace of historical figures like Franklin, Washington, Adams and Girard. Both the Declaration of Independence and the United States Constitution were drafted and approved in this neighborhood. And Bank Row on lower Chestnut Street became the nation's primary financial district—the first Wall Street, as it were.

The old part of town lost its standing as the city expanded in the 1800s. It became the commercial center of Philadelphia, filled with stores, hotels and light manufacturing. Well-heeled Quakers moved out and immigrants moved in. Many Old City residents left the area in the twentieth century as it evolved into a wholesale distribution center (focusing primarily on restaurant kitchen supply). By the 1960s, the worn-out district had completely outlived its usefulness for commercial/maritime activity, much like the bordering waterfront.

In 1971, the Philadelphia Planning Commission surveyed eight hundred warehouses and other structures and found that over half were decayed, vandalized or unoccupied. Following some favorable zoning changes, most of Old City's vacant and dilapidated nineteenth-century buildings were rehabilitated. Residents, retail and restaurants moved in where they had not been for a long time.

Today, Old City Philadelphia has over fifty restaurants serving every possible cuisine. Boutique stores provide shoppers with a wide range of choices, including the largest concentration of art galleries on the East Coast. All this is set in one of the country's greatest collections of cast-iron industrial loft buildings. The neighborhood's historical allure and its contemporary flair make Old City the place to see what's new in Philadelphia. A sometimes-boisterous crowd usually does so on Friday and Saturday nights.

Note that there's no *e* in Old City. "Olde City" is an affectation that started accidentally in the 1970s.

Ferries Crossing the Delaware (II of II)

Several railroads ran through New Jersey to coastal towns on the Atlantic Ocean, taking passengers to seaside resorts for a day, weekend or week of leisure. The railroads operated ferry routes plying from Philadelphia to Camden and other Jersey towns on the Delaware River. The ferry terminals of these railroads were concentrated near the Market Street Wharf.

The Pennsylvania Railroad's ferry unit was the Philadelphia and Camden Ferry Company, known far and wide for its fleet of eight steam ferries that transported passengers and vehicles to Camden's Federal Street Terminal. Walt Whitman, the Good Gray Poet, was a frequent user of this ferry, visiting from Camden to stroll around Philadelphia or to merely sit at the docks and watch people come and go.

The West Jersey Railroad, a subsidiary of the Pennsylvania Railroad, gained control of the Camden and Atlantic Railroad in 1883. Thirteen years later, the Pennsylvania consolidated its southern New Jersey lines into the West Jersey and Seashore Railroad. This is how the Pennsylvania Railroad wound up owning most of the ferry landings near the Market Street Wharf by the 1900s.

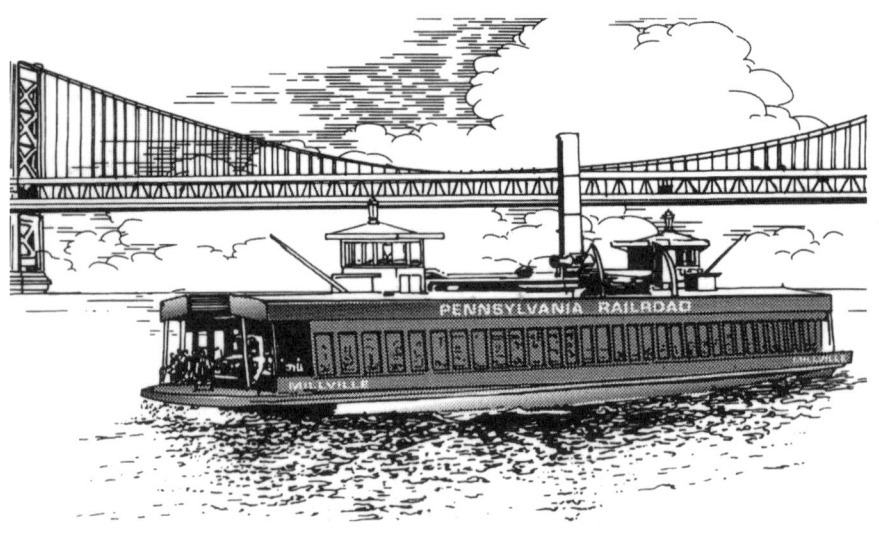

A ferry of the Pennsylvania Railroad's Philadelphia–Camden line. *Author's collection.*

At Market (High) Street

Delaware River ferries carried people, cars, trucks and busses well into the twentieth century. Over 100,000 passengers were transported daily at the height of ferry business in 1925. There was a departure from each side of the river every three minutes during peak periods. Over five million vehicles were carried at the apex of ferry activity.

The Benjamin Franklin Bridge and the assent of the automobile supplanted all the ferries that had crossed the Delaware since before the arrival of William Penn. This happened fairly quickly after the Second World War. The last regular Philadelphia–Camden ferry to operate was the Pennsylvania Railroad's, which held out until 1952—after 114 years of nonstop operation.

The bridge and the automobile also diminished railroad traffic between Camden and Atlantic City. The Depression did not help matters. So, in 1932, the Pennsylvania Railroad and the Reading Railroad joined their southern Jersey operations into one company, the Pennsylvania-Reading Seashore Lines. Service lingered on until the 1970s.

The Philadelphia and Camden Ferry's four-slip terminal's head house at the base of Market Street was built in the 1890s by the Pennsylvania Railroad.

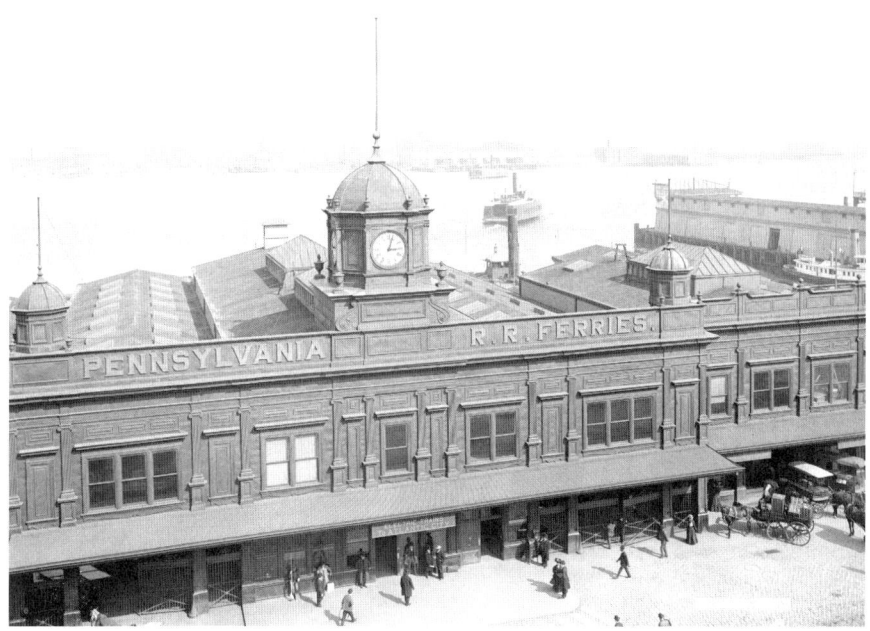

The Pennsylvania Railroad's Philadelphia–Camden Ferry Terminal about 1910. Picture taken from the Delaware Avenue El. *Library of Congress.*

This elaborate Victorian structure with a four-sided, clock-equipped cupola appears in many old photographs of Philadelphia's waterfront. It became a food market in the 1950s and was ultimately removed for the construction of Penn's Landing.

A lone tourist-oriented ferryboat between Penn's Landing and the Camden waterfront is a small connection to the past. This is the RiverLink Ferry, operated since the 1990s by the Delaware River Waterfront Corporation.

THE POLLUTED DELAWARE

In the heyday of ferry service, as many as 200,000 people would begin their annual trip to New Jersey's shore towns from the ferries on the central Delaware riverfront. Some would wait hours for the fifteen-minute ride across the channel. The trip was often unpleasant, as the Delaware had earned a reputation by the mid-twentieth century for being dirty and smelling bad.

Upstream industries had polluted the water to the point that longshoremen became ill from the smell of hydrogen sulfide. The shad that the Lenni-Lenape and others once harvested died in scores as the oxygen-depleted river itself died. Saturated with chemicals and other pollutants, the Delaware had not frozen over in a long time, let alone two feet thick as in the days when ice skaters and sleighs had a field day. It was so bad that paint would peel off the hulls of ships. People avoided being on or near the river unless they absolutely had to.

The Delaware River's industrial saga was much the same as that of Pegg's Run or Dock Creek (discussed later). Yet unlike those polluted local streams, the river was a beneficiary of the Environmental Revolution of the 1970s, becoming cleaner after federal and state environmental regulations took effect. Philadelphia's de-industrialization, for good or bad, also helped reduce water pollution in the Delaware. Shad and other fish have returned, and it's not unusual these days to see people fishing along the water's edge.

11
Market to Chestnut

Of Ancient Taverns and Franklin's Friends
on the Central Riverfront

Interspersed among the major streets of Old City are a number of charming alleys and courtyards with handsome commercial and residential structures from the nineteenth century. It's well worth wandering down Bank, Bread, Church, Cuthbert, Ionic, Quarry or Strawberry, all narrow and quaint in the Old Philadelphia way.

The Black Horse—Tavern and Steps

Black Horse Alley, an extremely narrow passageway a bit south of Market between Front and Second Streets, is an unnoticed alley of special interest. Originally called Ewer's Alley, it was renamed from the sign of a tavern later in the middle of that city block.

There were two Penn stairways between Chestnut and Market Streets. The northernmost one was the Black Horse Alley Steps, a continuation of Black Horse Alley. It's likely that these bank steps survived until the building of I-95, for they do appear on a 1962 Philadelphia Land Use map.

Also within the block is Letitia Street, once at the center of Letitia Court. This courtyard was intimately connected to the lore of William Penn. He reserved the whole city block for his personal use and then gave it to his daughter, Letitia, who later sold it off piecemeal. One parcel became home to the London Coffee House. The full story of Letitia Court is part of a larger tale too involved to convey here.

The Crooked Billet—Tavern and Steps

The other embankment staircase on this block was the Crooked Billet Steps, as it led to a tavern by that name on the Crooked Billet Wharf. This pier extended from Water Street onto the Delaware River roughly one hundred feet north of the bottom of Chestnut Street. The narrow space behind the tavern coupled with the wharf's irregular shape caused many people—maybe some inebriated—to fall into the river and drown.

Alice Guest arrived in Philadelphia in 1683 and began keeping a saloon in a cave on her bank lot facing the Delaware. Within ten years, she had built a wharf, warehouses and an inn: the Crooked Billet. This place was where Benjamin Franklin had his first hot meal and spent his first night in Philadelphia.

Watson reported that "[i]n 1721, the Grand Jury present, as out of repair and dangerous the Crooked Billet steps, above Chestnut street." What finally happened to these stairs is unknown, but they seem to have been closed in the mid-nineteenth century, whereupon the ground was likely taken over by neighboring property owners. These environs are all topped by Highway 95 today.

Philip Syng Jr. and Ben Franklin's Junto

Like carver William Rush, silversmith Philip Syng Jr. (1703–1789) was one of countless craftsmen who lived and worked along Front Street. He came to America in 1714 and later moved to this vicinity, where he obviously saw Benjamin Franklin around town. The two became friends. Syng helped Franklin with his electrical research and even made the static electricity machine with which the great scientist experimented in 1747.

Syng joined the Junto, the club of tradesman that Franklin organized in 1727 and which became the first discussion and intellectual club in America. The men of the Junto founded many of Philadelphia's longstanding public and private associations and organizations. They were familiar with the Delaware waterfront, as most lived and earned their livelihoods not far from the river.

Philip Syng designed and crafted an ornate silver inkstand for the Pennsylvania Assembly in 1752. It was this inkstand that members of the Second Continental Congress used to sign the Declaration of Independence and delegates to the Constitutional Convention used to sign the United States Constitution. Now part of the collection at Independence Hall, the Syng inkstand is surely (for what it's worth) the most important inkstand in the world.

Market to Chestnut

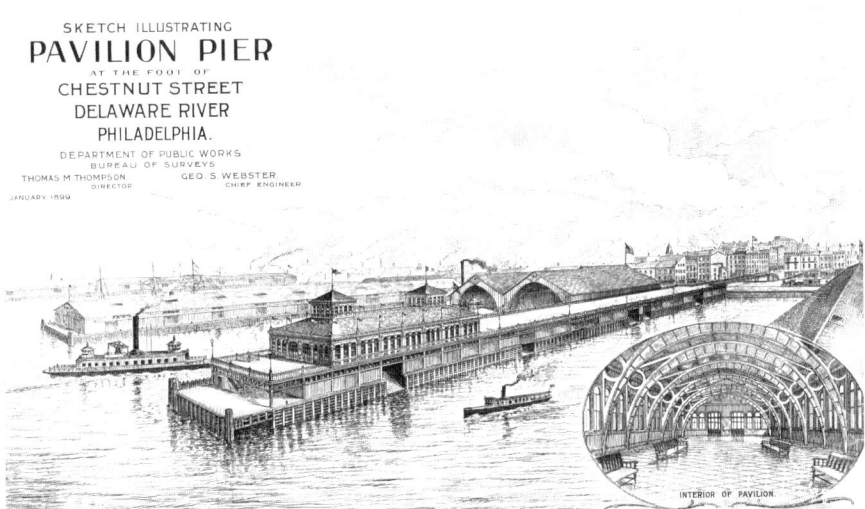

Plans for Chestnut Street Pier, with an inset showing the interior of the pavilion. *Philadelphia City Archives.*

THE CHESTNUT STREET PIER AND ITS NEIGHBORS

New finger piers were constructed between Market and Chestnut Streets after Delaware Avenue was enlarged to its current width by 1900. Pier 1 South was a covered timber-crib, earth-filled structure that was leased to a contractor for use in moving street dirt and ashes via barges. Pier 3 South processed fruit, grain and general freight for steamship lines trading to foreign and domestic ports.

Pier 5 South at Chestnut Street was owned by the city, which leased it to steamboat companies that handled food and wares. Built in 1899, Chestnut Street Pier had a steel superstructure and, like Race Street Pier, an ornate Victorian pavilion on its upper deck where people could relax by the Delaware. These public places were intended to act as parks alongside the river's edge.

A footbridge over Delaware Avenue provided quick access to the pavilion from the Market-Chestnut station of the Delaware Avenue El. The pavilion was removed in 1922 when Pier 5 South was modernized to become headquarters for the Department of Wharves, Docks and Ferries. Next to Pier 5 were ferry slips of the Delaware River Ferry Company of New Jersey, a service owned by the Reading Railroad.

Along with nearby warehouses, all the piers from Market to South Streets were removed in the 1960s to make way for Penn's Landing and Interstate 95 on this stretch of the river. The Philadelphia waterfront had become moribund by then, long past its prime as a commercial shipping district.

12

Chestnut to Walnut

A Welcoming Mansion (and Park) for William Penn Near the Birth of the Marines

Wynne Street, the first name of Chestnut Street, was taken from Thomas Wynne, William Penn's personal physician and a first purchaser of Philadelphia. Wynne's lot was at Front and Chestnut.

Samuel Carpenter's Wharf

Samuel Carpenter (1649–1714) was an English Quaker from Barbados, a friend of William Penn and a first purchaser. He had bought a small lot along the Delaware between Chestnut and Walnut Streets before coming to Penn's settlement. After his arrival in 1683, he constructed Philadelphia's first wharf there, along with a cottage overlooking the river.

Carpenter's Wharf was a notable landmark in the city's earliest days. William Penn wrote in 1683, "There is a fair key [dock] of about 300 foot square built by Samuel Carpenter to which a ship of five hundred tuns [tons] may lay her broadside." Gabriel Thomas states in his chronicle *An Historical and Geographical Account of the Province and Country of Pennsylvania* (1698), "There is also a very convenient Wharf called Carpenter's Wharf which hath a fine necessary Crane belonging to it." This cargo crane was widely praised in writings of the day.

The wharf was expanded over the years with numerous storehouses and other commercial structures, some of which stood for over a century.

Chestnut to Walnut

Carpenter's Stairs

William Penn conveyed a larger (204-foot-wide) bank lot to Carpenter on August 4, 1684, the day after issuing his decree that bankers could develop their riverbank property as long as they provided for public access to the Delaware River. This Carpenter plainly did. In an undated letter written that year, he informed Penn:

> *I am willing to make and maintain forever, 2 pair of stairs, viz., 1 pair from the water up to the wharf and the other from the wharf to the top of the bank, for the comodius passing and repassing of all persons to and from the water, free forever.*

And so were built Carpenter's Stairs, mentioned often in literature. The quote confirms that these steps began on the high river bluff and proceeded down past Carpenter's Wharf and into the Delaware itself. Carpenter's Stairs were on the line of Norris' Alley, later Gothic Street, a modest lane that subsequently became part of Sansom Street.

Sailors, merchants, servants and even slaves climbed Carpenter's Stairs for at least 125 years. Evidence suggests that they lasted until sometime between 1825 and 1847 and that the ground they occupied was incorporated into bordering property tracts. All of this ground is now covered by I-95.

Military Matters (II of V): Tun Tavern and the U.S. Marines

Samuel Carpenter and his brother, Joshua, opened the Tun Tavern brew house and inn at King (Water) Street and Tun Alley in 1685. (The old English word "tun" means a barrel or keg of beer.)

The first meetings of the St. John's No. 1 Lodge of the Grand Lodge of the Masonic Temple were held there in 1732. Benjamin Franklin was its third grand master. The Masonic Temple of Philadelphia recognizes Tun Tavern as the birthplace of Masonic teachings in America. Plus, the St. Andrews Society, a charitable group devoted to assisting Scottish immigrants, was founded there fifteen years later.

Tun Tavern was also, according to tradition, where the United States Marine Corps held its first recruitment drive. On November 10, 1775, the First Continental Congress commissioned Samuel Nicholas, a Quaker

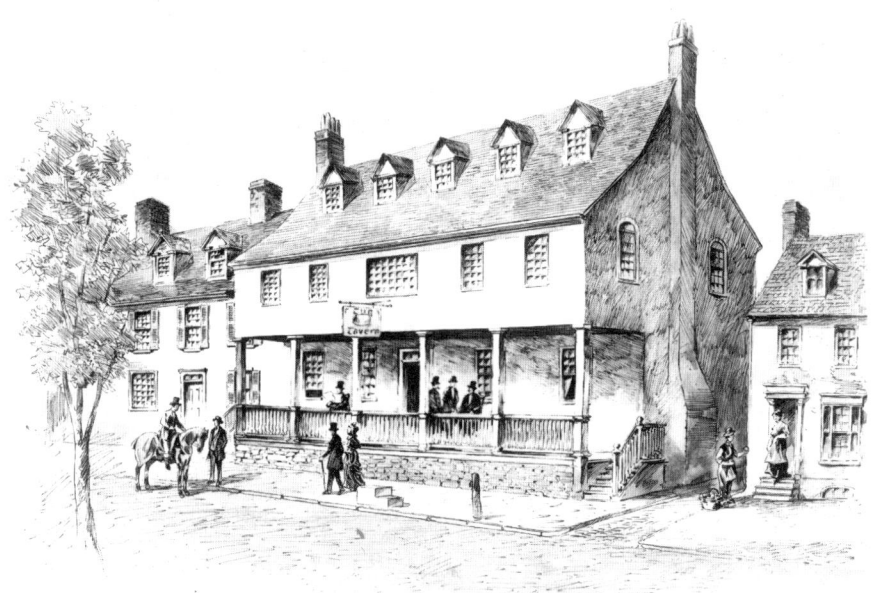

The Tun Tavern, by Frank H. Taylor. This drawing dates from about 1922, almost 150 years after the place burned down. *The Library Company of Philadelphia.*

innkeeper, to raise two battalions of marines in Philadelphia. The tavern's manager, Robert Mullan, was the head recruiter. Prospective volunteers flocked to the place, enticed by cold beer and the opportunity to join the new corps. The first Continental U.S. Marine unit was composed of one hundred Rhode Islanders commanded by Captain Nicholas. Some three million U.S. Marines have been exposed to the significance of Tun Tavern. Each year on November 10, U.S. Marines worldwide toast the place.

Fire destroyed the revered colonial inn in 1782. The Delaware Expressway covers the site nowadays.

City Tavern

Tun Tavern may be gone, but a reasonable facsimile stands at Second and Walnut. This is the City Tavern, a reconstruction of Revolutionary America's finest tavern.

The original City Tavern was put up in 1773 by a group of Philadelphia's most financially and politically prominent individuals who felt that the city deserved an excellent tavern, coffee shop and inn that reflected its status as the most cosmopolitan city in British North America. Merchants' Coffee House, as it was first called, was considered the best establishment of its kind in the colonies. Never one to over praise, John Adams called it "the most genteel" tavern in America.

City Tavern gained fame as the gathering place for members of the Continental Congresses and the Constitutional Convention and federal government officials from 1790 to 1800. The First Continental Congress initially gathered there before moving to Carpenters' Hall. The inn became Philadelphia's commercial center and stock exchange after the London Coffee House became too small and outdated for local businessmen.

Eclipsed as a center for business and politics, City Tavern was demolished in 1854 after a tragic fire involving a bridal party. The present structure is a faithful reconstruction by the National Park Service dating from 1975–76. It has since operated as an eighteenth-century-style tavern serving lunch and dinner daily.

Welcome Park and the Slate Roof House

Welcome Park is directly across Second Street from City Tavern. This urban courtyard presents a re-creation of Thomas Holme's 1682 map of Philadelphia, with the city's street grid laid in marble. A miniature version of the statue of William Penn that crowns Philadelphia City Hall stands on a pedestal in the center. Penn's plans and promotions for Philadelphia are illustrated on a wall enclosing the square, as is a timeline of his life. The place was named after his ship, *Welcome*, which brought Penn and over one hundred passengers, mostly Quakers, to America in 1682.

Welcome Park was dedicated exactly three hundred years later on the site of the Slate Roof House, the famed mansion that Penn used as a city residence during his second visit to America (1699–1701). It was there that Penn wrote and issued his "Charter of Privileges." This progressive framework for Pennsylvania's government became the model for the United States Constitution and is still the basis of free governments all over the world.

James Logan, the secretary of the Proprietary, also lived in the Slate Roof House and administered the colony of Pennsylvania from there between 1701 and 1704. The mansion became a crumbling object of interest prior to being taken down in 1867.

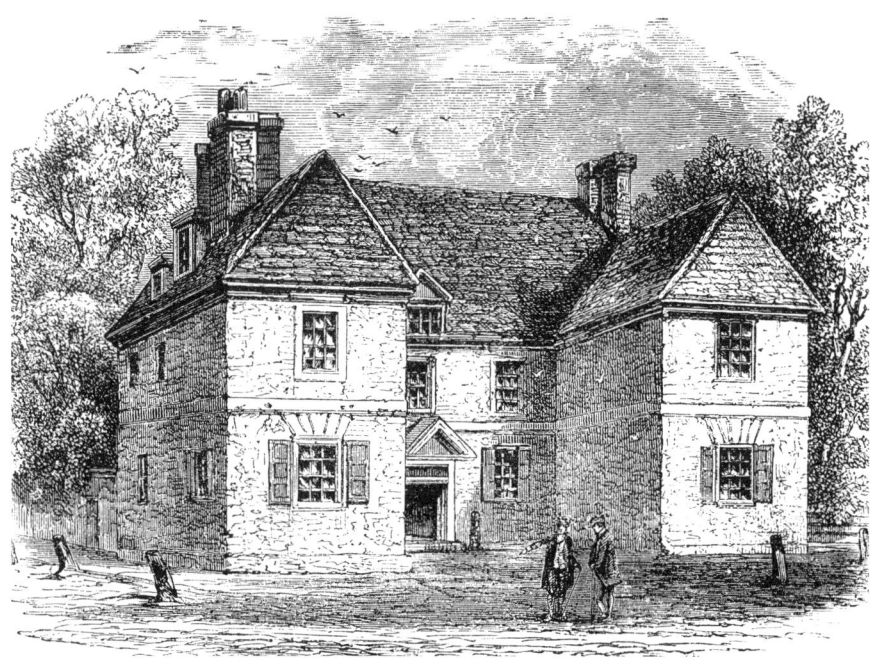

The Slate Roof House, today the site of Welcome Park. *Author's collection.*

It was Samuel Carpenter who built the Slate Roof House about 1687. He had acquired a large lot on the west side of Front Street all the way to Second Street. It was across from his original bank lot, where Carpenter later established Philadelphia's first coffeehouse, Ye Coffee House. He also opened the Globe Inn on this dockside lot. The tavern and the coffeehouse were separated by his bank stairwell.

THE WHARVES OF ROBERT MORRIS AND THOMAS COPE

These were just a few of Carpenter's many landholdings and business dealings in Philadelphia. He became the city's most successful and richest businessman—the Stephen Girard of his generation—and later entered into Pennsylvania politics.

Yet he was the first of several Philadelphia merchants who prospered on the riverfront between Chestnut and Walnut. Robert Morris (1734–1806), in his era, came to own the India Wharf along this frontage. (Morris is often called the "Financier of the American Revolution" for his financial dealings in support of the young nation during the Revolutionary War.) His ships and those of other merchant-financiers routinely left there for India and China. Goods imported from those exotic places were stored and sold at Morris's warehouse (called the Indian Stores) in front of the India Wharf.

Quaker merchant Thomas Pym Cope (1768–1854) moved his fledgling shipping business to the Walnut Street Wharf (also called Cope's Wharf) in 1810 and established a successful trade line between Philadelphia and Liverpool by 1822. Another early millionaire and philanthropist by the Delaware, Thomas Cope was both a tough rival and a trusted friend of Stephen Girard.

Old Original Bookbinder's

Another Samuel (besides Carpenter) made his mark on this block. Dutch immigrant Samuel Bookbinder had opened an oyster saloon at Fifth and South Streets in 1893 and five years later moved his popular eatery to 125 Walnut Street. There, he dished up all manner of seafood, getting his menu fresh off ships docked at the Delaware River. Shad, terrapin and oysters were favorite meals, and portions were generous to satisfy a very masculine crowd ranging from storekeepers and stockbrokers to sailors, sea captains and stevedores.

John Taxin bought the place in 1945 and renamed it Old Original Bookbinder's. During its zenith in the 1950s, '60s and '70s, waiters scurried through paneled rooms adorned with ship models, stuffed game fish and VIP photos. "Bookie's" became a mecca for celebrities, tourists and a regular crowd of Philadelphians. Personalities as diverse as the following always visited whenever they were in town: Howard Cosell, Muhammad Ali, Elizabeth Taylor, David Bowie, Gregory Peck, Julius Erving, John Wayne and Frank Sinatra. Even Madonna dined at Bookie's.

Anyone who was anyone came to Bookbinder's, including presidents of the United States. One day in 1972, the presidential helicopter landed in a parking lot across Walnut Street. (The food warehouses that had been there for ages had just been brought down, and the Sheraton Society Hill Hotel was not yet built.) To the astonishment of regular patrons, President Richard Nixon and Mayor Frank Rizzo had lunch at Bookie's that day.

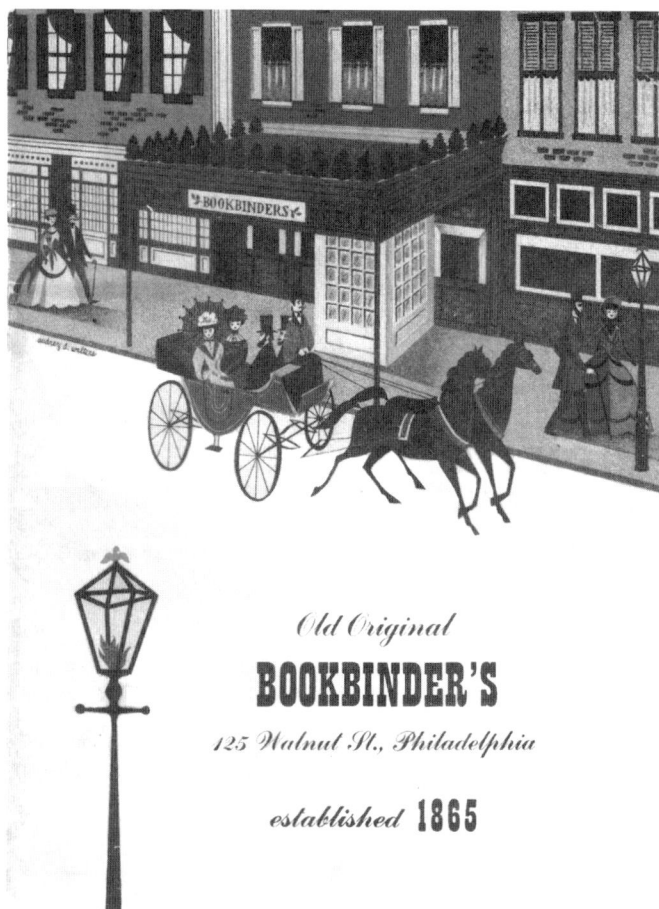

The cover of a booklet issued about 1960 to promote Bookbinder's Restaurant. *Author's collection.*

The venerable Philadelphia institution closed in 2001 due to financial difficulties and a series of fires. Bookie's reopened four years later after renovations and a new condominium complex attached in the rear, but the restaurant went bankrupt and closed for good in 2009. The set of buildings at 121–135 Walnut Street are now vacant.

13

WALNUT TO DOCK

Pirate Treasure, a Timeless Treaty, Troubled Taverns
and a Floating Church

Walnut Street was first referred to as Pool Street since it crossed a pool on a branch of Dock Creek close to Third Street. Walnut was cut off from Delaware Avenue when Highway 95 was built—a most unseemly consequence of the modern artery. However, a soaring bridge does carry pedestrians over both roadways to Penn's Landing.

Military Matters (III of V):
The U.S. Navy and the *Alfred*

If the United States Marine Corps can say it got its start at Tun Tavern, then the United States Navy can legitimately say it began a stone's throw away, at the foot of Walnut Street.

In November 1775, the Continental Congress purchased a four-hundred-ton vessel called *Black Prince* from Philadelphia's top merchant shipping firm, Willing, Morris and Cadwalader. (The "Morris" was Robert Morris.) This state-of-the-art ship had been launched the year before in Philadelphia. Congress chose Captain (later Commodore) John Barry to helm the vessel, which became the first flagship of the new Continental navy.

Barry re-rigged the ship as a twenty-gun light frigate renamed *Alfred*. This was the first warship on which a United States flag was hung. The mementous event occurred in December 1775 while the vessel lay in the

Delaware off the Walnut Street Wharf awaiting orders to sail. The flag was the "Grand Union flag," precursor to the Stars and Strips and considered the nation's first national flag. The *Alfred* had a brief but exciting career before it was captured by the British near Barbados in 1778.

Chapter sixteen will highlight the nation's first naval shipyard, established on Philadelphia's waterfront at the turn of the nineteenth century.

Doing Business on the Central Waterfront

Most business in Philadelphia was transacted all along Water and Front Streets on either side of High Street, but mostly on the south.

Robert Morris and other moneyed Philadelphians organized the Bank of Pennsylvania at City Tavern on June 17, 1780. This, the first public bank in the United States, was established on Front Street north of Walnut that July. Its purpose was to borrow money to purchase provisions for the Continental army. The Pennsylvania Bank was never a bank of general deposit, nor was it meant to be permanent. The Continental Congress reconstituted it in 1781 as the Bank of North America, the first corporate banking institution in the United States.

Customhouses, once the main generators of revenue for the United States, were located in all major seaport and river cities. Philadelphia's first U.S. Custom House was at Second and Walnut Streets in the early 1790s. It moved to Front and Walnut in 1795. From 1845 to 1935, the former Second Bank of the United States served as the Philadelphia Custom House. The federal government collected over half a billion dollars in customs revenue through the Port of Philadelphia in the first quarter of the twentieth century. The city's current federal customhouse is a striking edifice at Second and Chestnut constructed in the 1930s.

The American insurance industry began in this area as a consequence of all the foreign shipping and inland commerce conducted in Penn's City. On May 25, 1721, a printer named John Copson opened America's first marine and fire insurance company at his home on High Street near the docks. Until then, all underwriting for risks at sea and other maritime hazards originated in London. Copson was therefore the first insurance agent in America.

Furthermore, the first home of the Insurance Company of North America, now known as CIGNA and still based in Philadelphia, was at the southeast corner of Front and Walnut Streets beginning in 1795.

Walnut to Dock

The Merchants' Exchange

Many marine insurance companies had offices in the Merchants' Exchange, a neoclassic structure still standing at Third and Walnut. It opened in 1834 after a group of Philadelphia businessmen—including Stephen Girard just before he died—organized to build a proper merchants' exchange for the city. Designed by Philadelphia architect William Strickland, this was the first real trading edifice in the United States.

Real estate and mercantile transactions of all kinds transpired in the central Exchange Room as they preciously had at the London Coffee House and the City Tavern. Not surprisingly, some space was set aside for a coffee shop.

The Exchange Building's semicircular portico was an ingenious adaptation for the odd-shaped lot created by Dock Street. Strickland based its tower on the Choragic Monument of Lysicrates in Athens. It's said that this was because a local newspaper asserted in 1831 that "Philadelphia is truly the Athens of America." The tower allowed watchmen to scan the Delaware and

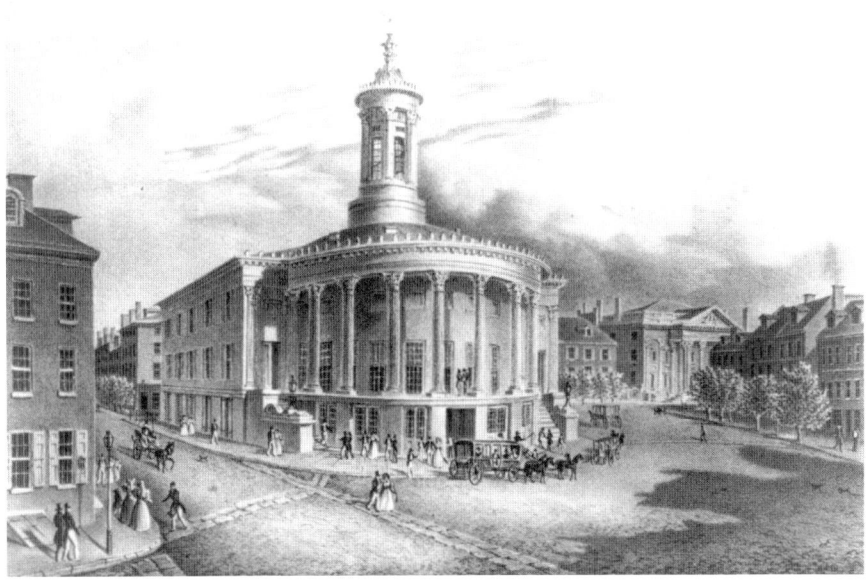

This 1830s print of The Merchants' Exchange also shows Dock Street on the right and Stephen Girard's Bank in the background. That building, formerly the First Bank of the United States, also still stands. *Library of Congress.*

notify merchants of ships approaching the city, much as Stephen Girard's servants had done from his mansion's high windows and roof. The tower on the Exchange Building today is a replica.

Originally known as the Philadelphia Exchange, this place was the country's financial center up until and during the Civil War. (The entire Northern war effort was essentially financed at this building.) Business activity about that time began moving west to the Broad Street corridor, so the Merchants' Exchange was refashioned as the Corn Exchange. Then, in 1875, it became home to the Philadelphia Stock Exchange. The stately building devolved into a food market surrounded by rickety sheds and produce trucks by 1922. Vendors hawked vegetables from pushcarts, and a gas station was built on the Dock Street side.

The National Park Service acquired the structure in 1952 and maintains offices there. A National Historic Landmark, the Merchants' Exchange is the oldest stock exchange building in America.

Working on the Central Waterfront

At least two sets of riverbank steps were south of Walnut Street. These were probably removed in the late 1800s to allow for the construction of commercial structures between Front and Water Streets. At the same time, long, wide freight depots and tall warehouses were erected—primarily by the Pennsylvania Railroad—in that zone east of Front Street.

These buildings serviced a grouping of finger piers and ferry landings owned by the railroad. Piers 10, 11 and 14 South were freight stations that handled coal, lumber and general merchandise carried across the channel to Camden in railroad cars on car floats. Over one hundred men worked at these wharves.

Between Chestnut and Walnut Streets, opposite Ton (Tun) Alley, was Pier 8 South, a covered timber structure owned by the Reading Railroad and used as a freight station for lumber, coal and general goods. Pier 8 was also the principal Philadelphia station of the Reading's Atlantic City division. This was where ferryboats connected with eastbound trains at Kaighn's Point in New Jersey. Next door was Pier 9 South, used by a river-transportation firm that employed barges to move gravel, lumber and general cargo.

The Merchants and Miners Transportation Company used Piers 16, 18, 20, 22 and 24 between Spruce and South Streets as private terminals in

Walnut to Dock

connection with passenger and freight service to ports in several states. When the Baltimore-based carrier was liquidated in 1952, roughly one hundred Philadelphia dockworkers lost their jobs.

Dock Creek—Dock Street

Dock Creek was a Delaware River tributary that provided a natural cove or tidal basin to early colonists. Hence its earliest name: the Dock. Called the "Coocanocon" by local Native Americans, it had three branches. The main one flowed northwestward to almost Sixth and Market. The second one went to Washington Square. The third, Little Dock, headed south to where Head House Square is today.

The creek was anticipated to have been a convenience to inland inhabitants of Philadelphia by affording easy transportation of food and goods into the interior of Penn's City of Brotherly Love. The tides regularly flowed inward as far as Chestnut Street, and the Coocanocon was navigable for sloops and schooners as far west as Third Street.

The mouth of Dock Creek was a swampy salt marsh skirted by a low sandy beach. A drawbridge was built to connect the north and south portions of Front Street over the inlet. Wooden bridges—later replaced with stone arches—were placed at Second, Third, Chestnut and Market Streets. Small ships with masts could pass under these spans at low tide.

Some pioneers lived in dugouts along the Coocanocon. The water was clean, the soil was grassy and the view of the Delaware was pleasant. Deer roamed nearby. As merchants flourished in Philadelphia, it became fashionable for them to build mansions on either side of Dock Creek, with lawns and gardens descending toward the banks. The Slate Roof House was one of these. When William Penn came down the Delaware from Pennsbury Manor in Bucks County to stay at the mansion, his boat would be rowed up the creek.

Breweries, lumberyards, slaughterhouses and tanneries were also built along Dock Creek. These industries discharged their putrid refuse into the stream, while the general public used it as a waste receptacle for chamber pots and the like. Like Pegg's Run, the tidal watercourse became polluted and sluggish.

The standing water of this open sewer became a civic concern and was blamed for a variety of public health problems. One of the earliest visitations of yellow fever in Philadelphia was supposed to have had its origin in the creek's filth. A good deal of controversy ensued, much of it cultivated by Benjamin Franklin in 1739, perhaps to initiate a public works project that would improve the city—or maybe just to sell his newspapers.

Dock Creek's main branch was culverted and paved over in sections beginning in the mid-1700s. The east part of the main branch was confined within stone walls and arched with bricks, while the western part and the secondary branches were filled in, all in keeping with a series of ordinances enacted over the years beginning in 1762. One in 1784 ordered the laying of paving stones to "form a public highway known by the name of Dock Street."

All this explains why Dock Street is a severely curved street in a city reputed for not having curved streets. Like Willow Street to the north, it follows the course of an old waterway. Dock Street was completed west of Front Street by 1821. The part between Front and the river was finished by 1839, when the first incarnation of Delaware Avenue was laid. Besides being curved, Dock Street is unusually wide (about one hundred feet), reflecting the original breadth of Dock Creek.

Dock Street eventually became Philadelphia's primary food market and served in that capacity for almost a century. As such, it became as dirty as

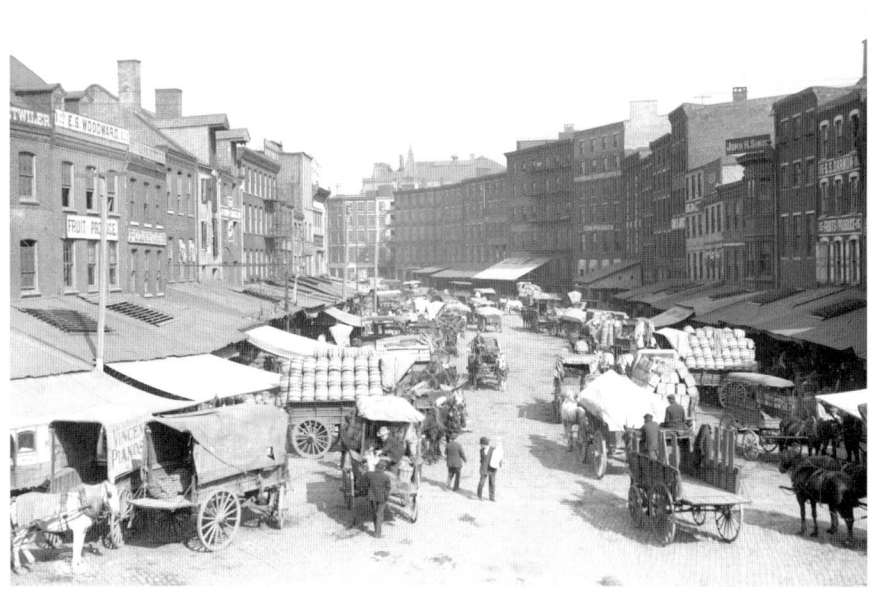

The crowded food distribution center on Dock Street about 1908. This was the street in its heyday. Trucks later made the scene even busier. *Library of Congress.*

Walnut to Dock

the creek it replaced. Grimy warehouses and market stalls with tin roofs over the sidewalk lined both sides of the Belgian-blocked street for decades. Food of all kind was unloaded from ships that docked nearby. Dock Street teemed with sellers and buyers and their horse-drawn wagons in the morning. By afternoon, it was deserted—except for the rats.

When larger motorized trucks replaced smaller wagons, the street was simply not able to handle the traffic. This state of affairs ended in 1959 when the sprawling Food Distribution Center opened on Packer Avenue in South Philadelphia. All the old food warehouses were torn down as Society Hill Towers and the Sheraton Society Hill took over Dock Street.

THE BLUE ANCHOR TAVERN

At the mouth of Dock Creek on the Delaware was the Blue Anchor Landing, which functioned as Philadelphia's main public wharf for decades. It was named after the Blue Anchor Tavern, a renowned inn that was under construction but already in business when William Penn first came to Philadelphia in 1682.

Penn arrived by barge from the downriver town of Chester, then called Upland. The tradition that he had a glass of ale at the Blue Anchor when he came ashore did not harm his standing among even the most pious members of the Society of Friends.

The Blue Anchor was a combination beerhouse, merchant exchange, grain market and post office. Its story was written by Thomas Allen Glenn and published in 1896 in the *Pennsylvania Magazine of History and Biography*:

> *For many years previous to William Penn's proprietorship there had been at Philadelphia (later so called) a constant landing of traders and of those inhabitants of West Jersey who were accustomed to go down to the sea in ships. The favorite landing-place was on the bank of the Delaware, between the present Walnut and Dock Streets, and it was directly back of this landing, on the higher bluff, that the Blue Anchor Tavern was subsequently built.*

> *The first building known as the Blue Anchor Tavern was of brick, was sixteen feet front by about thirty-six feet long, and stood directly in the middle of the present Front Street, then Delaware Front Street, about one hundred and forty-six feet north of Dock Creek, now Dock Street. In front*

of the Blue Anchor was the primitive wharf whereat Penn came ashore on his arrival from Chester, and which he erected into a public landing-place for the inhabitants of Philadelphia forever.

The saloon and its landing stood directly in the middle of the present Front Street, about 150 feet north of the former Dock Creek. This would be just a bit north of the current-day Dock Street. As the riverfront developed, the Blue Anchor moved to replacement structures closer to Dock Creek twice, the last time in 1690. This place was a house at the end of a line of row homes put up by builder Thomas Budd. The pub continued to serve fishermen and other customers until 1810, when it was taken down.

Many other taverns and coffeehouses for the benefit of seafaring men were located along this strip of the Delaware during the city's younger days. These establishments were more than merely places to drink and dine. They were where people transacted business, argued politics, got the news and otherwise socialized. Water Street linked them together, all the way to Penny Pot Tavern roughly a mile north.

The Man Full of Trouble Tavern

At Second and Spruce is a peculiar old Philadelphia pub that still stands: the Man Full of Trouble Tavern. First named the "Man Loaded with Mischief," it was built in 1759 along with the adjacent house. This is the only surviving pre-Revolutionary tavern in the city.

The widow Martha Smallwood managed the tiny place in the 1790s, as that was when Philadelphia authorities would award tavern licenses only to "widows and decrepit men of good character." That was also the time when there was one saloon for every fifty men in town.

The Man Full of Trouble was subsequently used as a hotel and wholesale chicken market, surrounded by other ramshackle houses and shops. The low-ceilinged building was on the verge of falling down before a private foundation restored it as a museum in 1965. Unfortunately, it's been closed to the public since 1996. At one time surrounded by unassuming buildings, the tavern now sits all alone—but with Society Hill Towers looming high above.

The amusing tavern sign outside the building depicts a dour sea captain with a monkey on his shoulder and a parrot on his hand, walking arm in

Walnut to Dock

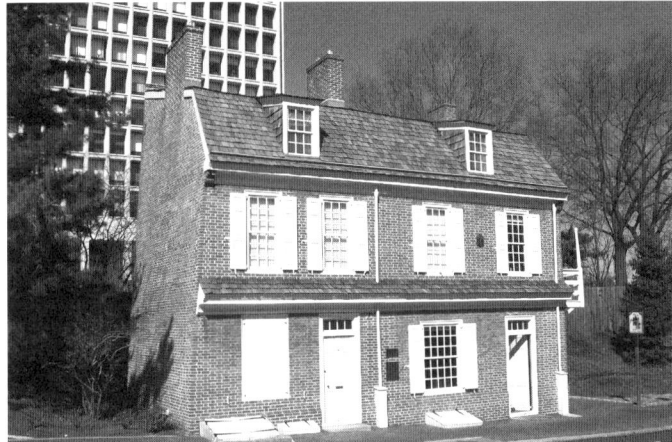

The closed but still standing Man Full of Trouble Tavern. The tavern itself is on the right. *Photo by the author.*

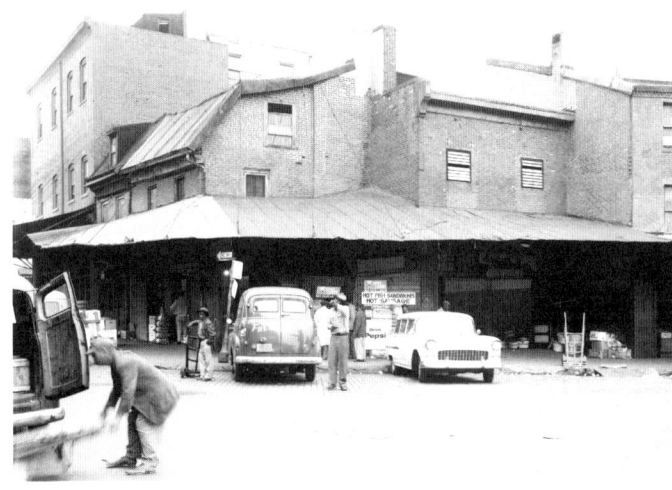

The Man Full of Trouble Tavern in 1958, when it was unrecognizable as a food wholesale place and surrounded by tattered buildings, much like itself. *Library of Congress (HABS).*

arm with a genteel lady holding a hatbox. The original sign featured a gaudy woman hoisting a glass of bubbly while carried on the sagging shoulders of an unhappy sailor.

PIRATES AND BURIED TREASURE

Besides the dutiful William Penn, the pirate Edward Teach (1680–1718), otherwise known as Blackbeard, was a patron of the Blue Anchor Tavern. Indeed, it was common to see pirates of the Atlantic Coast, including

Blackbeard and William "Captain" Kidd (ca. 1645–1701), openly swagger along Water Street and vicinity. Working and retired sea robbers liked being in Philadelphia because of the mild temper of Quaker justice.

But Penn, living in England at the end of the seventeenth century, did not endorse this. In 1697, he wrote to his American agent, William Markham—whose daughter married an alleged pirate—that Londoners maintained that Philadelphians "not onlie wink att but imbrace pirats, shipps and men." While the Pennsylvania Assembly denied this accusation, it did respond by passing a stringent law for the suppression of piracy and trading with or harboring buccaneers. But this did not halt Blackbeard's nefarious activities or his visits to Philadelphia. The same goes for other pirates.

Rumors of buried treasure along Philadelphia's waterfront persisted for hundreds of years. Watson claimed that a pot of money (at least $5,000) was once found buried in the cellar of a tavern at Front and Spruce Streets. Plus, many people hunted and dug for pirate plunder around where Fairmont Street met Front Street and also along Pegg's Run.

THE *FLOATING CHURCH OF THE REDEEMER*

The Seamen's Church Institute of Philadelphia was founded in 1843 to address the needs of both saints and scoundrels visiting ports on the Delaware River. The institute, now at 475 North Fifth Street, has had many offices over the years, but its first "building" was actually a boat—the *Floating Church of the Redeemer*. This unusual and impressive vessel was usually moored at the foot of Dock Street in the early 1850s.

Made in New York and dedicated on January 11, 1849, the floating Gothic church traveled up and down the Delaware River ministering to seamen whose ships were docked in the Philadelphia area. This was evidently the first floating church in the United States and apparently one of only three ever made. It was a venture of the Churchman's Missionary Association for Seamen, an arm of the Episcopal Church.

The wooden church, ninety feet long and thirty feet wide, rested on the hulls of two barges placed ten feet apart. With sailing flags waving from its seventy-five-foot steeple, it was deemed the most beautiful floating chapel in the world. The *Floating Church of the Redeemer* was so famous that a model of it was displayed at London's Great Exhibition of 1851.

Worshippers often left early due to seasickness, and the chaplain himself sometimes had trouble staying upright during services. The unpowered craft

Walnut to Dock

also tipped sideways in high winds and even sank once. By 1853, these problems and rising maintenance costs resulted in its sale. The floating church was towed to Camden, where it was hauled ashore and set on a brick foundation to become the landlocked Church of St. John's on Broadway Street.

A fire devastated the structure in 1868, but its bell is still in existence. Seamen's Church Institute now owns it after having found it via an e-Bay auction. The bell was missing for almost 150 years.

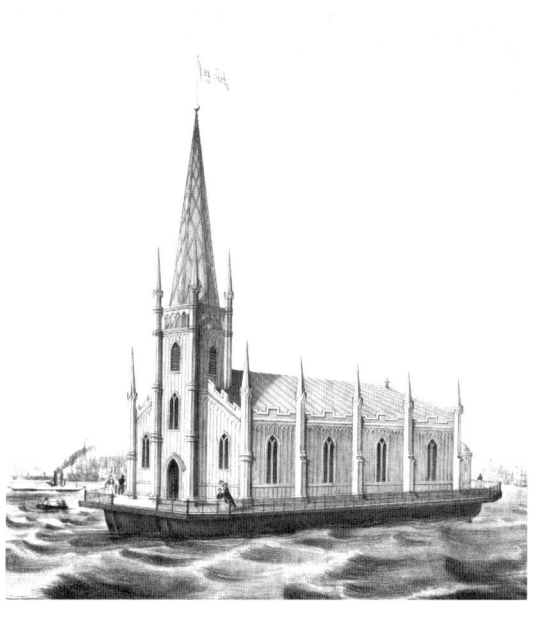

The *Floating Church of the Redeemer. Library of Congress.*

FOGLIETTA PLAZA

Thomas Glenn continued in his "The Blue Anchor Tavern" piece:

> At present the great wharves of the Pennsylvania Railroad Company cover the site, and a heedless crowd crosses constantly over the spot where the Founder first set foot on Philadelphia's soil. The curious, however, can still mark, in the grade of Water Street, at the distance of about one hundred and fifty feet north of Dock, a slight depression, which runs from the river to Front Street, marking, doubtless, the shelving bank which formed a pathway over which William Penn travelled from the landing to the Blue Anchor Tavern in the year 1682.

The "slight depression" is, of course, long gone, as is most of Water Street. Today, Dock Street from Front Street to Delaware Avenue is somewhat north of its original location owing to the upheaval caused by I-95. It was reconstructed atop the concrete cover above the superhighway, as was Spruce Street and Foglietta Plaza.

Little used and rather forbidding, Foglietta Plaza is administered by the Interstate Land Management Corporation. The little greenery of this maze-like courtyard hardly camouflages the ventilation towers and fire suppression equipment required for the tunnel underneath. And the incessant roar of vehicles speeding underground is distracting, if not deafening.

The plaza was named after Thomas Foglietta (1928–2004), an esteemed lawyer and Pennsylvania representative in the U.S. House from 1980 to 1997 (during which time he was involved with enhancing Penn's Landing and the Port of Philadelphia). Later an ambassador to Italy, Foglietta grew up a few blocks south of the plaza, on a street where his grandparents settled upon emigrating from Italy.

Foglietta Plaza lies squarely at the historic location of the mouth of Dock Creek, although the creek had long been buried by the time the courtyard was built. This spot was also the site of the Delaware Avenue Market, built in the mid-1800s and topped by a clock tower. This was the place to go to for fruit and vegetables, with heaps of watermelons, peaches, tomatoes and so forth on sale daily.

Incidentally, Front Street used to go straight through; it was not interrupted at Foglietta Plaza until the courtyard was installed when I-95 came through. So the plaza, in a way, represents how the drawbridge over Dock Creek connected the northern and southern segments of Front Street.

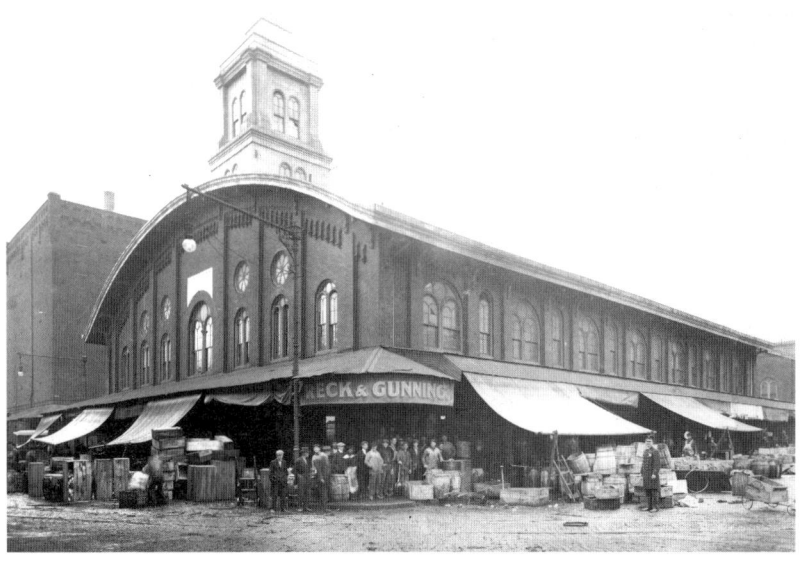

The Delaware Avenue Market at Dock Street in 1914. This building was torn down in the 1960s. Foglietta Plaza—atop I-95—occupies the space today. *Philadelphia City Archives.*

Walnut to Dock

MEMORIALS AT PENN'S LANDING

The Philadelphia Korean War Memorial is next to Foglietta Plaza. Dedicated on June 22, 2002, and again on October 7, 2006, after being enlarged, this reverential place pays tribute to the 610 servicemen from southeastern Pennsylvania killed or missing in action in the Korean War. The names of those who died are carved into four columns, while etched images on six granite walls portray the war itself. The memorial includes a bronze sculpture of a kneeling soldier, entitled *The Final Farewell*, by Lorann Jacobs.

Close by at Spruce Street is the Philadelphia Vietnam Veterans Memorial, on the concrete cover of Interstate 95. The monument remembers the 646 local residents who lost their lives during the Vietnam War. Scenes from the war and the names of soldiers killed in action are engraved on its two facing walls of polished granite. Dedicated on October 26, 1987, the memorial is sadly forgotten as a visitor's destination, largely because it is a secluded amphitheater. The Purple Heart Memorial, honoring men and women wounded in all American wars, is incorporated into the Vietnam Veterans Memorial.

Foglietta Plaza contains the Philadelphia Beirut Memorial, dedicated on October 20, 1985, to remember Philadelphia's U.S. Marine casualties of the Beirut Peacekeeping Mission killed in the terrorist bombing on October 23, 1983. And across Columbus Boulevard at the USS *Becuna* submarine is a memorial paying homage to Americans lost in World War II submarine combat.

THE LENNI-LENAPE AND WILLIAM PENN (II OF II): PENN TREATY PARK

These modern memorials have their antecedent in the monument that the Penn Society placed by the Delaware River at what is now Penn Treaty Park back in 1827. Still located there, this stone marker is, however, a monument to peace, not war. The Penn Treaty Monument commemorates the "Treaty of Amity and Friendship" between William Penn and local Indian leaders led by Chief Tamanend.

The extraordinary gathering occurred on June 23, 1683, under a giant elm tree (the "Treaty Elm") at Shackamaxon—an ancient Native American meeting place along the Delaware in present-day Northern Liberties/Fishtown. An interpreter read the deeds that Penn had prepared to the chiefs, who then made their marks. While the treaty itself was probably an informal

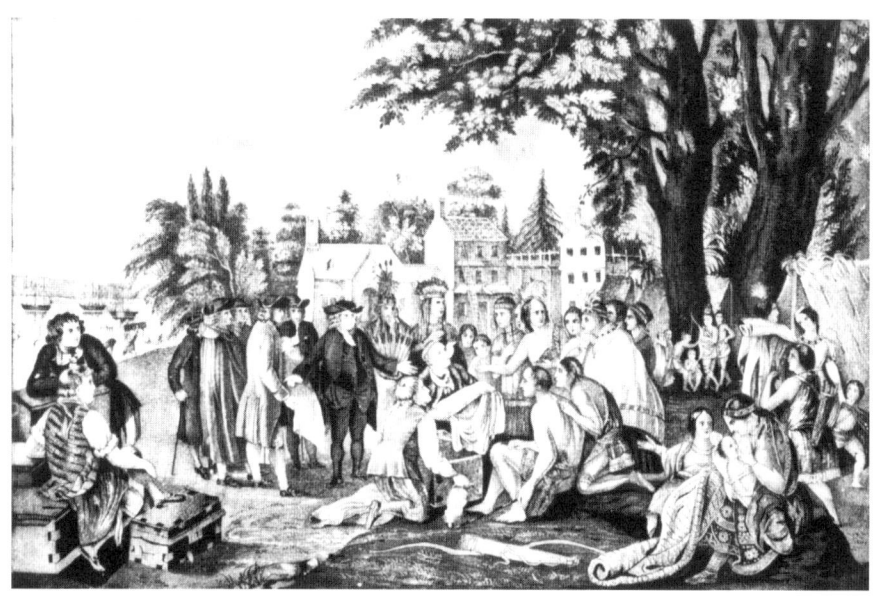

Wm. Penn's Treaty with the Indians, a Currier-Ives print from about 1845. This is one of countless views of the famous Treaty of Amity and Friendship made alongside the Delaware River between William Penn and local Lenni-Lenape leaders. *The Library Company of Philadelphia.*

unwritten pact, it was the primary reason why there was relatively little strife between the Quaker newcomers and the Delaware Indians living in the region.

Penn paid for Indian land with various goods, which Tamanend divided among his people. The chief then gave Penn a belt made of wampum beads as a sign of friendship. It featured a depiction of two men clasping hands: one large and with a hat (Penn) and the other smaller and hatless (a Native American). The Penn family kept this belt until 1857, when a descendant gave it to the Historical Society of Pennsylvania, which still has it.

The French philosopher Voltaire hailed the 1683 Treaty of Amity as "the only treaty between those nations and the Christian nations which was never sworn to and never broken." Its imagery—the Treaty Elm in particular— became a worldwide symbol of religious and cultural tolerance and an inspiration to the drafters of the U.S. Constitution.

Native Americans have always respected the location of this legendary event along the Delaware, handing down its story in their oral tradition. They have gathered on numerous occasions at Penn Treaty Park, which was officially established in 1893 as Philadelphia's first recreational park on the edge of the river.

14

Dock to South

Head House Square and a Progressive Sail Loft in Society Hill

These parts were called "South End" in the old days, just as the northern section of Philadelphia was called North End.

The Society of Free Traders

In 1682, William Penn chartered the Society of Free Traders to foster commercial development within his Pennsylvania settlement and maritime trade between Pennsylvania and England. The organization was basically a joint-stock company managed by a group of some two hundred affluent English Quakers to whom Penn turned for financial backing in establishing his colony.

The society purchased twenty thousand acres of ground in Pennsylvania and received a charter granting manorial rights, exemption from all quitrents and a choice of waterfront sites in Philadelphia. It also organized and dispatched some fifty ships to Pennsylvania and established a tannery, saw- and gristmills, a brick kiln, a glassworks and a fishery that actually caught dozens of whales (for the oil) in the Delaware Bay. (A beluga whale swam up the Delaware past Philadelphia as recently as 2005.)

While great results were expected, the society's influence diminished, and little came of its efforts. The company folded in 1723, in debt and having irritated many Philadelphia Quakers. Their chief complaint was that the Free Society received favorable treatment from Penn as to the best city plots.

One of those tracts was a 468-foot-wide swath of land between Spruce and Pine Streets from the Delaware River all the way to the Schuylkill River.

In a letter written in 1683, Penn described it to society members: "Your city lot is a whole street and one side of a street from river to river, containing near one hundred acres not easily valued." This territory included high ground overlooking and immediately south of Dock Creek, where the firm set up its local offices and storehouses.

This knoll became known as "the Society's hill." The name continued long after the demise of the organization itself.

In November 1739, Anglican Protestant George Whitefield preached fourteen sermons over a week from a platform atop the Society's hill. Several thousand people of all religious backgrounds came from far afield to hear the young field minister each day. His commanding voice was heard by men in boats on the Delaware and even two miles away in New Jersey. Whitefield returned the following April, and in later years, to preach from there and elsewhere in Philadelphia.

Benjamin Franklin attended a few of these revival meetings and wound up befriending Whitefield. Franklin was very impressed with the minister's ability to draw large crowds and with his speaking abilities. Whitefield's voice was so expressive that it was said he could move people to tears by how he pronounced the word "Mesopotamia."

SOCIETY HILL PHILADELPHIA

Society Hill started as a place where socially prominent people lived and worked, and it remained so through the mid-1800s. Then the region lost its cachet as the center of Philadelphia moved west. By the 1950s, Society Hill was a slum that predominantly housed poor immigrant families. Noted preservationist Charles Peterson (1906–2004) said that it was a "has-been neighborhood" when he moved there in 1954.

But starting in 1958, the Philadelphia Redevelopment Authority embarked on an enormous urban renewal project for the precinct. The city acquired crumbling Georgian and Federal houses via eminent domain and sold them to buyers who agreed to restore the buildings according to certain standards. In this way, about six hundred eighteenth-century houses were renovated. Nineteenth- and twentieth-century structures that did not "fit in" were replaced by contemporary houses that sought to combine colonial tradition with modern style.

City planners chose the appellation "Society Hill" to honor the locality's heritage. The district became a true urban redevelopment success story, filled with

Dock to South

charming row homes, tree-lined streets and sidewalks of brick and cobblestone. Once again a prestigious neighborhood, Society Hill contains the largest concentration of original eighteenth- and early nineteenth-century architecture anywhere in the United States. Its renaissance sparked the similar revitalization of Old City, Queen Village (Southwark) and the rest of Center City Philadelphia.

SOCIETY HILL TOWERS

The three Society Hill Towers are skyscraper condominiums located between Walnut and Spruce Streets, above Dock Street and interrupting Second Street. Designed by I.M. Pei and Associates, they were completed in 1963 and represented a very different type of building than those in the then-dilapidated Society Hill district. The towers embodied the rebirth and rise of this quarter, replacing dozens of run-down food warehouses from when this region was Philadelphia's main food distribution hub.

Society Hill Towers have become one of the finest residential centers in the world. Perched on a substantial hill (symbolizing the Free Society's hill) and each thirty-one stories high, they would have made a very conspicuous landmark for Philadelphia-bound seafarers in the old days. The complex consists of 624 units, many of which provide some of the best views of Center City and the Delaware River.

This was a rental community until a condominium conversion in 1979. The development includes modern ground-level housing that goes well with the eighteenth-century homes throughout the neighborhood. Modern sculptures embellish the five acres of landscaped grounds.

The neighboring Sheraton Society Hill Hotel was built in the Colonial style and has a four-story atrium lobby. Developed by Rouse and Associates, the hotel opened on July 4, 1986. Over 130 prehistoric Native American artifacts were recovered on the triangular site during an archaeological study before construction.

NEW MARKET AND HEAD HOUSE SQUARE

In 1745, ground in the middle of Second Street from Pine to Cedar (later South) Streets was designated as a marketplace for the South End's growing population. Market stalls were raised, and the place was named New Market to distinguish it from the High Street Market. A head house at Pine

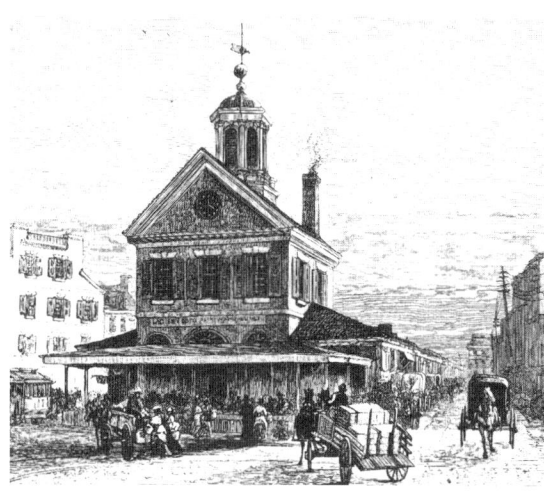

New Market's Head House in the nineteenth century. From History of Philadelphia, 1609–1884 *(1884)*.

Street was built in 1804–05 for use as a meeting place for volunteer fire companies and other associations and for the storage of fire apparatus. Another head house had been erected earlier at South Street but was taken down in 1860.

The market sheds were commonly called the "Mid-Street Markets" and the "Second Street Markets." They were also referred to as the "Shambles," an old English word for meat markets or butcher shops. Operating into the twentieth century, this covered open-air bazaar was presumably the country's oldest public market before it fell into ruin in the mid-1950s. In 1962–63, half of the Shambles—between Pine and Lombard—was rebuilt to replicate its eighteenth-century predecessor. The Head House at Pine Street was also restored.

The Head House and shed now signify the heart of Society Hill and provide a venue for community events. The re-created Shambles can still claim to be the oldest market in continual use in America, since it's still used as a farmers market selling locally grown produce. Artists and craftsmen occasionally display their wares there too. Meanwhile, the Head House is said to be the oldest firehouse in the United States.

Declared a National Historic Landmark in 1966, the two-block plaza is called Head House Square nowadays. Shops, cafés and restaurants line both sides of Second Street, many occupying rehabilitated buildings from Philadelphia's colonial past. Comprising some ten acres of historic properties, Head House Square was listed as a historic district on the National Register of Historic Places in 1972.

Dock to South

JAMES FORTEN AND HIS SAIL LOFT

James Forten Sr. (1766–1842) lived and labored in this neighborhood—the east end of Lombard Street. Becoming one of the richest African Americans in America, he was born free in Philadelphia and was educated in Anthony Benezet's Quaker-inspired Negro School at Philadelphia.

Forten was apprenticed in his youth to Robert Bridges, a sailmaker who had a sail loft on a wharf at Front and Lombard. Bridges was pleased with Forten's work and promoted him to foreman overseeing some three dozen employees. With Bridges' help, Forten purchased the shop in 1798. It was unusual for any novice to take over the business where he learned his trade, but it was especially rare for a black apprentice to take charge of a successful white-owned enterprise.

About this time, Forten purportedly began experimenting with different types of sails and perfected one that made ships maneuver easier and achieve greater speeds. He did not patent his invention, but he was able to profit from it since his sail loft became one of Philadelphia's most prosperous maritime businesses. Forten's $300,000 life's fortune would make him a millionaire today—another one along the central Delaware.

James Forten was also an abolitionist and a reform leader well before Fredrick Douglass came on the scene. Not only was his sail shop integrated, but Forten also financed a range of antislavery activities. He purchased the freedom of slaves, opened a school for black children and even established an Underground Railroad stop at his home.

The site of Forten's sail loft is now within the footprint of Highway 95. Interestingly enough, the workshop was located a few steps away from where abolitionist Francis Pastorius once lived in a comfortable cave by the water.

The waterfront from Pine to South Street about 1800, showing James Forten's sail loft business at center right. *From* Philadelphia and Her Merchants *(1860).*

15

South of South Street

Southwark Hosts a Swedish Church and a Party for the Ages

South Street was labeled Cedar Street when Philadelphia was first planned, but people soon started calling it by its present name because it formed the city's (original) southern limit. In the 1960s, South Street became known around the country as "the hippest street in town" thanks to the rock 'n' roll hit "South Street" by the Orlons. ("Where do all the hippies meet? South Street, South Street.") The South End was cheerfully bohemian back then as it is today.

But trouble was brewing. The Crosstown Expressway, discussed for years, would have obliterated a block-wide swath of the city along South Street from the Delaware to the Schuylkill Rivers. Mayor Frank Rizzo finally canceled this monstrous project in 1974, but the hip street still took a terrible hit as residents and businesses moved away in anticipation of construction. The neighborhood managed to recuperate after the project's termination and South Street again became a trendy promenade with unconventional boutiques and restaurants.

Speaking of unconventional restaurants, the Caledonia Tavern was once on the south side of South Street near Front Street. According to Watson, this was "a great place of resort for Scotchmen" and "had a swinging sign on one side of which was a picture of two friends shaking hands." The motto beneath was "May we never see an old friend with a new face."

South of South Street

Wicaco/Southwark/Queen Village

South Street is part of the Queen Village neighborhood, bounded approximately by South Street, Washington Avenue, Sixth Street and the Delaware River. This is Philadelphia's oldest and best-preserved precinct, as well as the first part of the city to have been settled by Europeans.

In 1669, fur-trading Swedes established a hamlet in this area, which the Lenni-Lenape called "Wicaco" (pleasant or peaceful place). Wicaco (Wicacco/Weccacoe/etc.) was an outpost of the New Sweden colony on the lower Delaware River.

Land by the river was occupied by the Swedish family of Sven, whose log cabin stood on a knoll at what is now the northeast corner of Beck and Swanson Streets. The structure stood for more than a century until British troops used it as firewood during the Revolutionary War.

Wicaco ultimately became the Southwark District of Philadelphia County and then the Southwark section of the city. The name was adopted because of its location south of Philadelphia, an allusion to the similarly situated English borough on the Thames just south of London. The streets and alleys of Southwark on the Delaware sustained a diverse group of artisans, tavern keepers, mariners, shipbuilders, shopkeepers and farmers. Whole blocks developed seemingly overnight in the 1800s.

But like Society Hill and Old City, Southwark hit hard times in the twentieth century. Local real estate agents dubbed the area "Queen Village" in the 1970s to help improve its image and to acknowledge the community's colonial roots. The term venerates Queen Christina of Sweden, who encouraged Swedish colonists to settle the land. Some local holdouts still refer to these environs as Southwark.

Queen Village was the first Philadelphia neighborhood to offer modern housing on the river side of the Delaware Expressway. This is the Court at Old Swedes development at the end of Christian and Queen Streets. Dozens of town house condos were built in the early 1980s on the site of a Pennsylvania Railroad freight yard. The land had previously been a shipyard, that of Simpson & Neil. More new housing is being built there today.

Conversely, the narrow three-story abodes at Front and Carpenter are some of the oldest row houses in Philadelphia. These eighteenth-century workers' houses are called "trinities" (Father, Son and Holy Spirit) because they typically had only one room per floor. New residents of Queen Village have restored many of these humble homes to their original appearance. But alas, about 130 were condemned and pulled down for the building of I-95. The trinities that remain shake when trucks speed by on the elevated freeway slicing through these parts.

Water Street was offset at Pine Street and was known for a time as Penn Street. Another street closer to the Delaware was put in and was first called Larkin Street, then Little Water Street and finally Swanson Street. Like the small houses, corner bars and mom-and-pop grocery stores standing alongside them, most all of these little streets gave way to the Interstate.

Military Matters (IV of V): The Sparks Shot Tower

Sterling Helicopter operates Philadelphia's only public-use heliport at Pier 36 South, once a Reading Railroad property.

A potential hazard to local helicopter pilots is the Sparks Shot Tower, an unusual structure on the 100 block of Carpenter Street. Towers like this revolutionized the making of musket balls, based on the principle that molten lead will form perfectly round droplets while falling from up high. Firewood and lead were taken to the top of the tower, where a furnace was fired to melt the lead. Poured through perforations, the lead would spin into balls that hardened upon hitting pans of water on the ground.

This was one of the first shot towers in the United States, opening in 1808. Thomas Sparks, John Cousland and John Bishop raised the 142-foot-tall structure to turn out shot for sport purposes. But tons of ammunition were produced there during the War of 1812. Bishop, a pacifist Quaker, accordingly sold his share of the business to Sparks as a result of the change in production to purposes of warfare. The factory later produced shot during the Civil War. Four generations of the Sparks family kept the place running into the early 1900s. It was also called the Southwark Shot Tower and the Philadelphia Shot Tower.

Resembling a lighthouse or factory chimney, Sparks Shot Tower is thirty feet in circumference at its base and tapers to fifteen feet at the top. It acted as a landmark for ships coming up the Delaware River for many years, much as Christ Church steeple did. The structure is now part of a city playground with a gymnasium at its base. An excellent example of Philadelphia's reputation for superb brickwork, this is one of the last towers of its kind in the world.

South of South Street

Gloria Dei (Old Swedes') Church

Gloria Dei (Glory of God) Church is at Christian Street and Columbus Boulevard. Its "Old Swedes'" nickname stems from the church's founding members being Swedish Lutherans who came to Wicaco from what is now Wilmington, Delaware.

A log blockhouse (a small fort) fronting the Delaware River was renovated as a place of worship in 1677 and was used until the present church was completed in its place in 1698–99. Gloria Dei was consecrated on July 2, 1700, making it the oldest house of worship in Pennsylvania and the second-oldest Swedish church in the United States.

This was the site of the first regular Lutheran ordination in North America. Justus Falckner (1672–1723) was ordained there in 1703 to serve Lutherans in New York. The first recorded use of an organ in any American church was at Gloria Dei for Falckner's ordination. Famous Philadelphians, such as Betsy Ross, were married at this church, and its cemetery contains the graves of notable early Americans, including John Hansen (president of the Continental Congress under the Articles of Confederation), Alexander Wilson (poet and "Father of American Ornithology") and five of General Washington's officers.

Old Swedes' has been an independent institution of the Episcopal Church since 1845. It is owned and administered as the Corporation of Gloria Dei Church by a small congregation that maintains the property and oversees a collection of relics. Affiliated with the National Park Service as a component of Independence National Historical Park, the church was designated a National Historic Landmark in 1942 and was listed on the National Register of Historic Places in 1966.

The old church house is a resilient colonial survivor, wedged, as it is, between Interstate 95 and Columbus Boulevard. Although it sits east of a segment of Water Street (originally Ostego Street around here), Old Swedes' was not built on made-earth. It was constructed long before "making earth" on the Delaware's west bank became all the rage.

Gloria Dei thrives in spite of being so close to I-95 and being separated from its historic Southwark neighborhood, much of which the expressway destroyed. The highway's routing was first proposed to be closer to the river, where it would have passed directly outside the church's front windows—assuming that the church itself would not have been eliminated.

The Mischianza

Joseph Wharton (1707–1776) was a member of a well-known Philadelphia family who prospered enough as a cooper to become a "gentleman." In 1731, he bought a sizable tract in Southwark and gave the name Walnut Grove to the country house he built there. His estate had a long front yard that sloped all the way to the Delaware River, the equivalent of three city blocks away.

On May 18, 1778, Walnut Grove was the scene of the Mischianza (or Meschianza), an Italian word for medley or miscellany. This was an extravagant ball given in honor of British general William Howe during the occupation of Philadelphia. Howe, commander in chief of British forces during the early years of the Revolution, had resigned his post and was about to return to England. Twenty-two of his officers threw the ball, which was masterminded by Captain John André, a future British spy.

A parade of fifteen decorated boats with over four hundred invitees departed from a wharf in Northern Liberties. Conveyed on the Delaware to Southwark, the guests included: Admiral of the Fleet Richard Lord Howe, the general's brother; General Henry Clinton, Howe's replacement; Peggy Chew, daughter of Quaker lawyer Benjamin Chew; and Peggy Shippen, future wife of Benedict Arnold.

The Mischianza's festivities included a seventeen-gun salute by British warships, a tournament of jousting knights, three musical bands, a banquet and a fireworks display. One month after the fourteen-hour affair, some seventeen thousand British troops evacuated Philadelphia, having accomplished little—except throwing a great big party—during their occupation of Penn's City of Brotherly Love.

The Southwark Group Piers

Two huge warehouse piers, Piers 38 and 40 South, jut 551 feet into the Delaware River at the bottom of Christian Street. Jointly known as the "Southwark Group," the brightly painted piers date from 1915 and are each 357,000 square feet in size. They were once the city's busiest docks. For instance, international shipper Norton, Lilly & Company operated an around-the-world cargo service from Pier 40 in the 1920s. Vessels would travel twenty-seven thousand miles between visits to homeport Philadelphia.

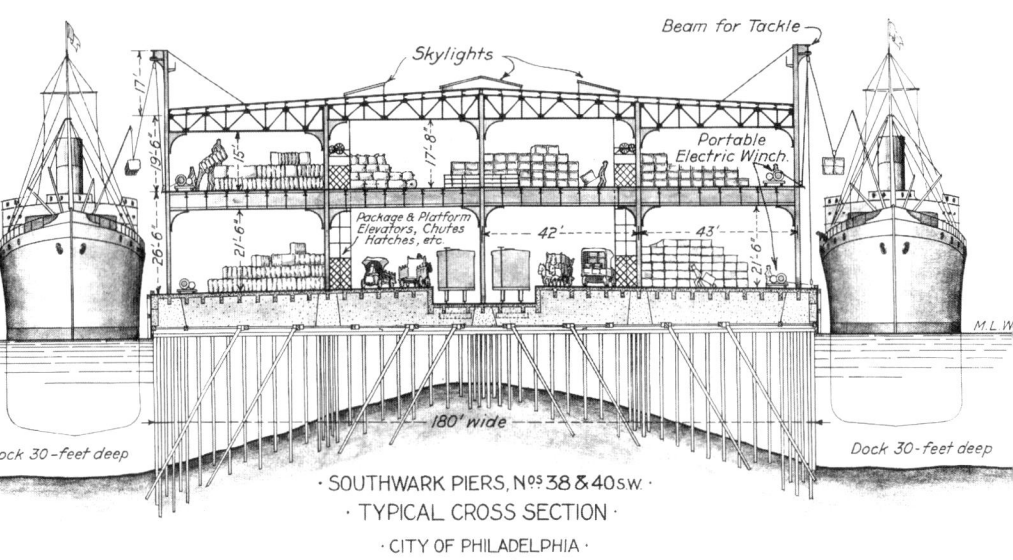

Cross section of the Southwark Group piers. Most early twentieth-century piers in Philadelphia were built like this. *Philadelphia City Archives.*

In the 1950s, the space between Piers 38 and 40 was filled in and paved to accommodate tractor-trailers. The buildings are used for warehousing these days, including a self-storage business. Few boats ever tie up to the Southwark Group Piers anymore.

16
AT WASHINGTON AVENUE

Fortress to Shipyard to Navy Yard to Rail Yard to Immigration Station to Waterside Park

Love Lane was the early name for the eastern end of Prime Street, which is now called Washington Avenue. John Watson said that the lane was long ago shaded on both sides with large sycamore trees.

THE BONNIN AND MORRIS WORKS (AMERICAN CHINA MANUFACTORY)

The second porcelain works in America was located on the west side of Front Street just south of what is now Washington Avenue. English émigré Gousse Bonnin (ca. 1741–ca.1778) and Philadelphian George Anthony Morris (ca. 1742–1773) partnered to establish the American China Manufactory in 1769–70. They wanted to prove that colonial Americans were capable of turning out high-quality domestic goods. The plant's proximity to the Delaware was necessary for the water-intensive process of making porcelain.

The Bonnin and Morris Works specialized in attractive blue-and-white tableware based on stylish English prototypes and often mistaken for English porcelain. They announced the first successful production of their wares in early 1771. But their business operated fitfully due to financial problems, foreign competition and disputes with the English and European potters they employed. One of the many early industries that lined Philadelphia's Delaware waterfront, the American China Manufactory closed in 1773.

At Washington Avenue

Still, the firm had made some of the rarest porcelain museum pieces in the world. Certain items include a painted capital *P* (for Philadelphia or Pennsylvania), which is the earliest known maker's mark of any kind on American pottery or porcelain.

The works on Washington Avenue subsequently became an artillery (cannon) factory. Row homes now occupy the spot. Philadelphia's Mummers Museum is close by at Second and Washington. This part of the city is called Pennsport.

MILITARY MATTERS (V OF V): THE ASSOCIATION BATTERY

Speaking of artillery, the first fortification to defend Penn's City was the Association Battery, located at the foot of what became Washington Avenue. Unlike the British barracks at Campington, this was a fort—and a locally inspired one at that.

When hostilities arose between France and Great Britain in 1744, the Quaker-led Common Council of Philadelphia refused to take steps for the city's defense. Consequently, Philadelphia and its merchant fleet were under threat of attack by French and Spanish privateers sailing up the Delaware. Benjamin Franklin, who argued for the common defense of Philadelphia in his political pamphlet *Plain Truth* (1747), finally roused the public into action.

Franklin and his cohorts formed a military "association"—the Association for General Defense—on December 7, 1747. This was Pennsylvania's first citizen militia and predecessor of the Pennsylvania National Guard. Hundreds and hundreds of men volunteered to become "associators." Ben Franklin was virtually in command of this corps, despite having declined a commission.

The Common Council petitioned the Pennsylvania Propriety to supply arms and ammunition, which the colonial government promised if Philadelphians raised the money to build the fort. Without delay, Franklin and his Junto colleagues organized a lottery. The Association Battery (aka the Grand Battery) was erected in 1748 on a hill near Gloria Dei Church. It first mounted twenty-seven guns (cannons) and later held some fifty. Rudimentary drawings of the fort show three buildings enclosed by a crenellated stone wall rising about fifteen feet.

The Association Battery was Pennsylvania's largest early fortification but was never called on to defend Philadelphia. During the Revolutionary War, the

British mounted guns there and built another battery and a redoubt nearby, all of which were used against American ships sailing on the Delaware. The Grand Battery fell into decay after the war and the eleven-acre site became the shipyard of master shipbuilder Joshua Humphreys in 1794.

Shipbuilding (III of III): Joshua Humphreys' Shipyard

Apprenticed to a Philadelphia shipbuilder in his youth, Joshua Humphreys (1751–1838) was a ship designer during the War for Independence and helped draw up plans for the Continental navy frigate *Randolph*. The tragic story of the USS *Randolph* is too lengthy to tell here, but it is enough to say that this vessel, launched in Philadelphia on July 10, 1776, is regarded as the first true warship of the United States.

Humphreys was appointed as the first chief naval constructor of the United States in 1794, when Congress passed an act providing for the production of six frigates. Larger and faster than other warships of their class, they were the inception of the U.S. Navy and formed the core of American naval forces during the War of 1812. Each of these brilliantly designed sailing ships was made at a different port in the new nation. William Rush carved figureheads for four of them at his Front Street workshop.

The first vessel was the USS *United States*, built at Humphreys' Southwark yard. Visitors from all around walked through the shipyard at will, observing the three-masted ship's construction. Joshua Humphreys personally led President George Washington and First Lady Martha on a tour.

The *United States* was the first American warship launched under the U.S. Constitution, as well as the first American frigate and the first naval vessel christened "United States." Authorized by President Washington as Commission No. 1, it was launched on May 10, 1797, and began a splendid career under Commodore John Barry's command. The highlight of its service was the capture of the British frigate *Macedonian* on October 25, 1812.

Decommissioned in 1849 and placed in reserve at Norfolk, Virginia, the USS *United States* was seized in 1861 and commissioned into the Confederate navy as the CSS *United States*. The ship was scuttled in the Elizabeth River to form an obstruction to Union vessels, but Union forces raised it. The gallant old frigate was broken up for scrap wood in 1865.

At Washington Avenue

THE FIRST PHILADELPHIA NAVY YARD

The federal government purchased Joshua Humphreys' shipyard for $37,000 in 1800–01. This was the first location of the Philadelphia Navy Yard, the first naval shipyard of the United States and the foremost building and outfitting plant of the U.S. Navy Department for seventy-five years. Its two towering ship houses were the most eye-catching structures on Philadelphia's riverfront for years.

Important fighting ships took to the water here, notably the *Dale*, *Franklin*, *Lancaster*, *North Carolina*, *Princeton*, *Raritan*, *Susquehanna*, *Vandalia* and *Wabash*, all destined to have a part in the nation's naval history. William Rush carved the figureheads for some of these vessels.

The most famous was the USS *Pennsylvania* (1837). One of nine ships authorized by Congress in 1816, it was designed by Samuel Humphreys, Joshua's son. The 120-gun *Pennsylvania* was the biggest and most heavily armed man-of-war built up to that time. About 100,000 spectators—some on some two hundred boats on the Delaware—gathered to watch its long-awaited launching on July 18, 1837. The *Pennsylvania* eventually wound up at the Norfolk Navy Yard, where it was burned in 1861 to prevent it from falling into Confederate hands.

Another distinguished ship of the Philadelphia Navy Yard was the USS *Mississippi*, launched in 1841. America's first sea steamer and the longest ship then in the American navy, the *Mississippi* became the first steam-powered U.S. naval vessel to reach the Far East when it served as Commodore Matthew Perry's flagship on his historic 1852 expedition to Japan. The *Mississippi* went under at Port Hudson, Louisiana, on March

Currier-Ives print of the ship-of-the-line USS *Pennsylvani*a, completed in 1837 at the first Philadelphia Navy Yard. *Library of Congress.*

14, 1863, when its magazines exploded after it was set ablaze to prevent capture by Confederates.

A new ship is customarily christened before being put into the water, a ceremony that involves giving it a name and breaking a bottle of wine on it. Until October 22, 1846, only men had christened American naval vessels. But on that date at the Southwark yard, a "Miss Watson of Philadelphia" became the first woman to christen a warship (the USS *Germantown*).

This shipyard had the world's first floating sectional dry dock, constructed in 1851 at a cost of $830,000. The structure had nine wooden pieces, each one 32 feet wide, 105 feet long and drawing 10 feet of water. When used together, they had a displacement lift of fifty-eight hundred tons and could accommodate vessels 1,000 feet long. Ships requiring repair would be rested on the dry dock's floor when it was filled with water. A sliding cradle was positioned under the keel, and a hydraulic cylinder would slide it and the vessel onto slipways. This is much more intricate than the launching ramps James West employed at his shipyard a century before.

When U.S. naval ports in the South fell to Confederate forces during the Civil War, the Philadelphia Navy Yard stood as the Union's first line of naval defense. It was the main supply and repair yard for the North Atlantic Blockading Squadron, responsible for blockading the Confederacy's coastline. Moreover, this yard converted and outfitted more than one hundred warships during the war, including a number of ironclads.

By then eighteen acres, the cramped shipyard became even more packed with the special fabrication shops and equipment needed to put together these new vessels. The place needed to expand, but surrounding development in Southwark precluded this. More significant was the fact that the success of ironclad warships made wooden warships—the yard's specialty—instantly obsolete.

In 1876, the U.S. Navy had moved the facility to open space at the confluence of the Delaware and Schuylkill Rivers in South Philadelphia. There, a sprawling new shipyard was laid out, and the Philadelphia Navy Yard entered its second glorious phase of American history.

Washington Avenue Immigration Station

The Pennsylvania Railroad took over the Washington Avenue site when the Navy Yard departed. There, the railroad built extensive freight yards east of Front Street on both sides of Washington Avenue. This was a lively place

At Washington Avenue

from the 1870s through the 1920s, with a robust grouping of factories, grain elevators, sugar refineries, storehouses and shipping piers centered on the rail yard and Delaware Avenue.

The Pennsylvania Railroad also opened Philadelphia's first immigrant station at a pier in conjunction with the American Line Steamship Company. The Washington Avenue Immigration Station off Pier 53 South became a key point of entry for Eastern and Southern Europeans and was rivaled only by Ellis Island in New York City.

Between 1870 and 1915, millions of newcomers began their journeys into America from Philadelphia's Southwark quarter. The Pennsylvania Railroad's tracks on Washington Avenue led to Pennsylvania's coal counties and the steel industries in other parts of the state. The tracks also took immigrants toward the American Midwest and beyond.

Other immigrants, mostly Italians, tended to settle close by, thus giving South Philadelphia its special flavor and reputation for being an Italian enclave. Some went to work at the various wharves and shipyards along the Delaware. Others found employment in any number of local factories at a time when Philadelphia was the Workshop of the World.

A municipal immigration station was also at the Vine Street Pier (Pier 19 North). Other privately-owned stations were on the wharves at Callowhill and Reed Streets. These sites are critical for understanding Philadelphia as a major immigration port and for appreciating how bordering neighborhoods became home to successive waves of German, Irish, Slovak, Italian, Polish and Jewish migrants.

In the early 1900s, Congress began funding new immigrant stations around the country so as to lessen the traffic at Ellis Island. The Washington Avenue Station was demolished in 1915 with plans to build a larger replacement. World War I and immigration restrictions of the 1920s prevented this from happening and brought an end to fifty years of direct migration to the Port of Philadelphia.

Pier 53 and the Life and Death of an Old Commercial Pier

Pier 53 South was the site of a spectacular fire on June 15, 1965. Aided by tugboats, six fireboats and some three hundred firemen put out an impressive blaze fueled by the pier's wooden construction and drums of oil stored inside. Ships tied alongside the warehouse pier were scorched and dockworkers trapped on the far end had to jump onto tugs to avoid the flames. The conflagration leveled the seven-hundred-foot-long structure.

As told in chapter three, what happened to Pier 53 happened to many of the old and abandoned wharves along the Delaware in the 1950s, '60s and '70s. They had timber frames and were clad with galvanized metal, so it's not surprising that they burned so readily. The items they stored made them even more susceptible to fire—particularly arson—if they were little used or vacant.

Other piers collapsed into the river, which is what occurred with the far end of Pier 34 South in 2000 (discussed in chapter nineteen). Following a fire or collapse, only the timber poles that once supported the pier's deck were all that usually remained after debris was removed. Many of these pilings can still be seen on either side of Penn's Landing at low tide on the Delaware.

Washington Avenue Green and the Delaware River Trail

The Sheet Metal Workers' Training Center sits on the site of the Washington Avenue Immigration Station.

The United States Coast Guard Station Philadelphia is next door. Its area of responsibility encompasses the second-largest freshwater port on the East Coast. The Delaware River in the vicinity of Philadelphia has both recreational boaters and hulking commercial vessels sharing the waterway. This dual use of the river presents unique safety and security concerns for the Coast Guard.

Other ground formerly part of the Pennsylvania Railroad's rail yard here has been transformed into Washington Avenue Green. Built in 2010 on a sea of concrete and asphalt, this is the first public space established by the Delaware River Waterfront Corporation. The atypical ecological park includes a rain garden, a "rubble meadow" and floating wetlands. Like Race Street Pier, it provides Philadelphians with a new respite on the Delaware and serves as a tribute to William Penn's desire for Philadelphia to be a Greene Countrie Towne.

Washington Avenue Green is accessible via the Delaware River Trail, a multi-use pathway along the river from Washington Avenue south to Pier 70 Boulevard. To the north, this trail incorporates the Riverwalk path created in the 1970s to connect major activity points along the central waterfront.

The Delaware River Trail will one day link to the trail planned for the entire western edge of the Delaware River. This trail will ultimately become part of the East Coast Greenway, a three-thousand-mile path from Maine to Florida.

17

WATER (KING) STREET

A FILTHY STREET TRIGGERS THE YELLOW FEVER EPIDEMIC OF 1793

Water Street was laid down alongside Philadelphia's waterfront in the mid-1690s and perhaps as late as 1705. Early settlers first called it "the street under the bank." It began as an uneven footpath, then turned into a muddy cartway and finally became a paved—with cobblestones and then Belgian blocks—lane. It was first named King Street, supposedly because goods crossing over it one way or the other had to pay a duty to the king of England.

In the seventeenth and eighteenth centuries, communities founded by the English up and down the Delaware River (and in other places) often had waterside streets named "King" and "Front." King Street's name was changed to Water Street about the time of the American Revolution, for understandable reasons.

REGULATION OF THE BANK OF THE RIVER DELAWARE

Following William Penn's return to England in 1684, the growing demand for land along the Delaware's edge—and the correlating opportunity for profit—caused the Commissioners of the Proprietary to issue patents for larger bank lots on the east side of Front Street.

While these land grants restricted the height of structures that could be built on the embankment lots, they still ran counter to the policy that Penn established in 1684 regarding the bank lots. Furthermore, the *Minutes of the Board of Property of the Province of Pennsylvania* contain more than a few complaints against bankers who did not follow Penn's directives in one way or another.

Then, in 1690, Samuel Carpenter and neighboring bankers presented Penn's agents with a petition that sought "full and free liberty to build as high as they please above the top of the [bank of the Delaware], which they were not to do by a clause in the said rexive [recited] former Patents." Their rationale for wanting to "build as high as they please" on Front Street toward the river was that "the more their improvements are" in elevation or value, "the greater will be the Proprietor's benefit at the expiration of said fifty-one years, in the said Patents mentioned."

The fifty-one years refers to a stipulation in some land patents that required the lots and their improvements (i.e., buildings and the like) to be appraised by two mutually chosen men after fifty-one years, with one-third of the appraisal to be paid to the Propriety on the first day of every March thereafter. Carpenter and his neighbors wanted to get rid of this provision in particular, substituting it for a small sum of money to be paid to the Propriety at that moment.

Penn's commissioners acquiesced. The agents approved the petition and formulated the "Regulation of the Bank of the River Delaware," an act executed on April 26, 1690.

John Watson recorded that James Logan wrote a letter to Thomas Penn about all this in 1741. Logan's letter read:

> *Thy father himself acknowledged when* [last] *here* [1699–1701] *that he owed* [as a cause] *those high quit-rents for the Bank lots of Philadelphia, and the reversion of the third of the value* [ground and all] *after fifty years, entirely to Samuel Carpenter, who, against his* [Penn's] *will had tempted him… to suffer himself* [Carpenter] *and other purchasers in the* [Delaware] *Front to build on the East side of that* [Front] *street.*

Watson continued:

> *Thus, even Penn, who should have had his equivalent for so essential a deformity engrafted upon this city, after all, got not the proffered benefit of fifty years accumulation of value in houses and lots, but a small present sum in lieu; and we have now the entail of their selfish scheme! I feel vexed and chagrined, while I pen this article, to think for what mere personal purposes fair Philadelphia was so much marred!*

Water (King) Street

―◆―

How mortified and vexed must Penn have felt on his second arrival in 1699, to witness the growing deformity of his city, and to see how far individual interest had swerved his agents from the general good!

Watson points out that William Penn did later realize that things had gone amiss and that Carpenter and his fellow bankers had taken advantage of the situation. Penn sent new directives to his Philadelphia agents, including the following in 1703: "I will have no more bank lots disposed of, nor keys [docks] yet made into the river, without my special and fresh leave, for reasons justifiable." But by then it was too late to correct the problems that had ensued since 1690.

Nevertheless, William Penn's initial attempt (in 1684) to resolve the Delaware riverbank dilemma was moderately successful, since it ensured that commerce and maritime activity would expand in Philadelphia by allowing goods to be easily moved to and from visiting ships. And it helped secure a connection—however slight—to the Delaware River for all Philadelphians.

The "Street Under the Bank"

The 1690 "Regulation of the Bank" instrument formally authorized and established what eventually became Water Street. Bank lot owners were instructed to "regularly leave thirty feet of ground in the clear, for a cartway under and along the said whole Bank," which was to become "a common and public cartway for all persons by day and by night, forever hereafter." It was up to the individual landowners to clear the ground, install a hard surface and provide drainage.

And what a busy street the street under the bank was in the 1700s!

Watson wrote: "An aged lady, S.N., told me, that in her youth the ladies attended balls held in Water street, now deemed so unfit a place!" It seems that a dancehall was inaugurated in 1748 at a wharf on Water Street between Walnut and Dock. This was the initiation of Philadelphia's famed Dancing Assembly.

In 1754, Lewis Hallam (the "Father of the American Theater") and a troupe of London actors performed for two months on Water Street, just north of Lombard. This may have been the first legitimate theater in Philadelphia. The venue was a brick storehouse owned by William Plumsted, mayor of the city from 1750 to 1755. Hallam remodeled the place and called it the New Theater. Resistance by neighboring Quakers shut it down.

The first theatrical company to appear in Philadelphia probably used this Water Street warehouse years earlier, in 1749. The troupe—by the name of Murray & Kean—reportedly staged Joseph Addison's *Cato*, although *Richard III* may also have been performed, maybe for the first time in the New World. Quaker authorities promptly ran this traveling group out of town.

An actual lion was exhibited for a couple weeks at "Abraham Bickly's new store in Water Street." This was in September 1727; admission was one shilling. The lion—the first in North America—was exhibited in several cities throughout the 1720s. Bickly (or Bickley) was a member of the Provincial Council of Pennsylvania who lived within walking distance of his storehouse and wharf on Water Street.

CONTAGION BY THE DELAWARE (II OF II): THE YELLOW FEVER EPIDEMIC OF 1793

Notwithstanding its cultural and entertainment aspirations, Water Street was the prime breeding ground for disease in Philadelphia. Scourges (e.g., malaria and typhus) had always made their initial appearance along Water Street from the city's founding until the early 1900s.

The most infamous outbreak in the city's history was the horrendous yellow fever epidemic of 1793. Sweeping outward from the congested neighborhood around Water and Arch Streets, this plague claimed the lives of some four thousand people, about 10 percent of the city's population at the time. Philadelphia's yellow fever epidemic of 1793 is still regarded as the worst urban disaster in United States history.

In late summer, as the number of deaths began to climb, twenty thousand citizens fled to the countryside, including George Washington, Thomas Jefferson and other members of the federal government, then based in Philadelphia.

Stephen Girard chose to stay. He contributed money to help victims of the epidemic and performed the duties of a nurse when the plague was at its worst. He volunteered to manage the temporary municipal hospital at Bush Hill, changing it from a dirty hellhole into a clean and efficient infirmary. Girard even used his own carriage to transport stricken people to Bush Hill, which was at about Eighteenth and Spring Garden Streets. In doing these things, he risked his life for no perceptible personal gain.

Water (King) Street

Early on, Mayor Matthew Clarkson asked the College of Physicians of Philadelphia to call a meeting of local doctors to determine what to do. This was the first time in American history that a government entity asked a medical organization to investigate a healthcare matter. Sixteen college fellows convened but could offer no solution for the contagion. These great scientists and doctors—who had made Philadelphia the medical capital of America—simply did not realize that the mosquitoes swarming around the city were transmitting the disease from person to person. These mosquitoes happened to be most plentiful along the Delaware waterfront.

Recall Dr. Benjamin Rush's hypothesis, which he proclaimed widely, that rotting coffee at the Arch Street Wharf was the epidemic's source. The doctor's supposition was wrong, but it may have prompted Mayor Clarkson to order city scavengers to clear out the streets and gutters, starting with Water Street. This did not help.

After three months of misery in Philadelphia, the plague subsided when the weather cooled in the fall and the mosquitoes died. Yellow fever reappeared in subsequent years, however.

Not much changed in those subsequent years in terms of the state of Water Street. The following is an account—from Isaac Weld, *Travels Through the States of North America* (1799)—of the cartway's still-dismal condition at the turn of the nineteenth century:

> [Water Street] *is the first street which you usually enter after landing, and it does not serve to give a stranger a very favourable opinion either of the neatness or commodiousness of the public ways of Philadelphia. It is no more than thirty feet wide, and immediately behind the houses, which stand on the side farthest from the water, a high bank, supposed to be the old bank of the river, rises, which renders the air very confined. Added to this, such stenches at times prevail in it, owing in part to the quantity of filth and dirt that is suffered to remain on the pavement, and in part to what is deposited in waste houses, of which there are several in the street, that it is really dreadful to pass through it.*

Water Street had not improved in fifty years, as the following from *Yellow Fever, Considered in Its Historical, Pathological, Etiological, and Therapeutical Relations* (1855) attests:

> *For many years after the settlement of the city, this street, on both sides, was thickly inhabited by the better classes of people; but for some time past, the*

houses have been in a great measure converted into stores or shops, while the balance are tenanted by the poorer and lower orders—sailors, emigrants, &c. As may be presumed, from its situation under a high bank, its mode of construction, the use to which it is appropriated, its proximity to the river, the character and number of its occupants, this street is far from being kept in that state of cleanliness so necessary to the preservation of public health; and is withal imperfectly ventilated.

Stephen Girard's Will (II of III)

Water Street's filthiness must have bothered Stephen Girard a great deal. After all, he lived and worked along the lane for much of his life.

As noted before, Girard left the City of Philadelphia half a million dollars for enhancing the Delaware's western edge. His will directed that water pipes, pumps and fire hydrants should be installed along Water Street from Vine to South Streets "to conduct the water through the main streets and the centre alleys to the river Delaware" for the purpose of cleaning the streets and the bank step alleyways. These improvements were most certainly carried out, but it's unknown if Water Street was ever regularly flushed as Girard had desired.

Almost all of this storied street in Philadelphia's central waterfront was obliterated in the late 1960s/early '70s for Highway 95's construction. A few blocks of Water Street survive between Summer and Callowhill Streets. Another segment remains behind Gloria Dei Church, although this was formerly Ostego Street. And a fragment of Water Street exists at the rear of the High Pressure Fire Service building at Race Street.

Delaware Avenue (Columbus Boulevard)

Lost Resort Islands and Girard's Riverside Legacy

Delaware Avenue was first an irregular footpath next to the river, built atop covered-over and filled-up docks and piers that had outlived their usefulness. Over time, though, it became a more formal thoroughfare, thanks to Stephen Girard.

Stephen Girard's Will (III of III)

Girard specified in his will that a wide boulevard should be constructed along the Delaware:

> *XXII. *** 1. To lay out, regulate, curb, light and pave a passage or street, on the east part of the city of Philadelphia, fronting the river Delaware, not less than twenty-one feet wide, and to be called Delaware Avenue, extending from Vine to Cedar* [South] *street, all along the east part of Water street squares, and the west side of the logs, which form the heads of the docks, or thereabouts;… to compel the owners of wharves to keep them clean, and covered completely with gravel or other hard materials, and to be so levelled that water will not remain thereon after a shower of rain; to completely clean and keep clean all the docks within the limits of the city, fronting on the Delaware.*

Philadelphia's Lost Waterfront

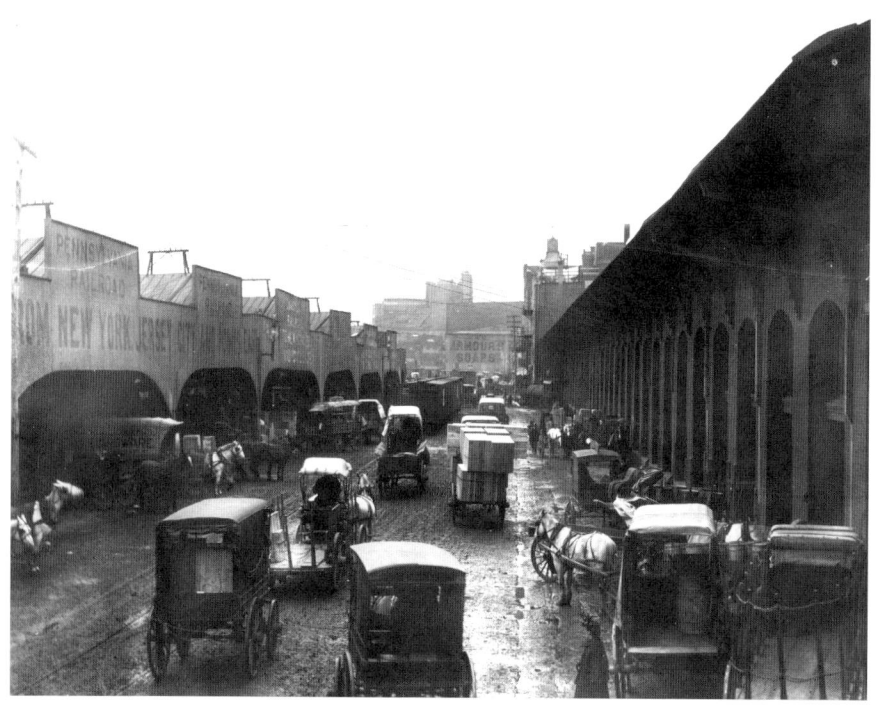

Delaware Avenue in 1898, before its last widening, looking south at Walnut Street. The Pennsylvania Railroad's freight depot is on the right; its wharves are on the left. *Philadelphia City Archives.*

Note that Girard explicitly labeled this boulevard "Delaware Avenue." His requirement that the roadway be "levelled [so] that water will not remain thereon after a shower" must have been followed to the letter, as Delaware Avenue is one of the most level streets in the city.

The Pennsylvania General Assembly passed an act on March 24, 1832, authorizing the city of Philadelphia to carry out Girard's wishes. The funds he left the city first allowed for extending the primitive pathway beside the Delaware eastward into the river, incorporating existing docks and using landfill (made-earth) to make the roadbed. The project took place between 1834 and 1845.

The work produced Delaware Avenue, a proper street twenty-five feet wide and paved with Belgian blocks between Vine and South Streets. Girard's money also led to the construction of bulkheads and the first lighting along the river (first with gas lamps, later with arc lamps). The City of Philadelphia expended $249,696.81 of Girard's legacy.

Delaware Avenue (Columbus Boulevard)

With Delaware Avenue so close to the water, the bowsprits and booms of ships sometimes extended over to storehouses on the avenue's west side. This is much like how parts of the front of vessels at James West's shipyard would reach over Water Street one hundred years earlier.

Commerce increased rapidly, and the city had to undertake the second widening of Delaware Avenue from 1857 to 1867, this time to fifty feet. The work expended $313,726.30 from Girard's Delaware Avenue Fund. The avenue was also extended north of Vine and south of South Street in the 1870s and successively afterward.

Traffic tie-ups continued to increase, a state of affairs that often delayed shippers who hauled perishable goods. So additional widening occurred from 1897 to 1900, when Delaware Avenue was broadened to 150 feet. This street became the widest and longest riverside avenue in the world.

The 1890s work was the most expensive civic improvement project in Philadelphia up to that time. Wharf owners were, of course, compensated for their property and buildings, as they had been during earlier widenings of Delaware Avenue.

A new concrete bulkhead line was also constructed for a mile alongside the river to allow for larger and more up-to-date shipping terminals. Today's

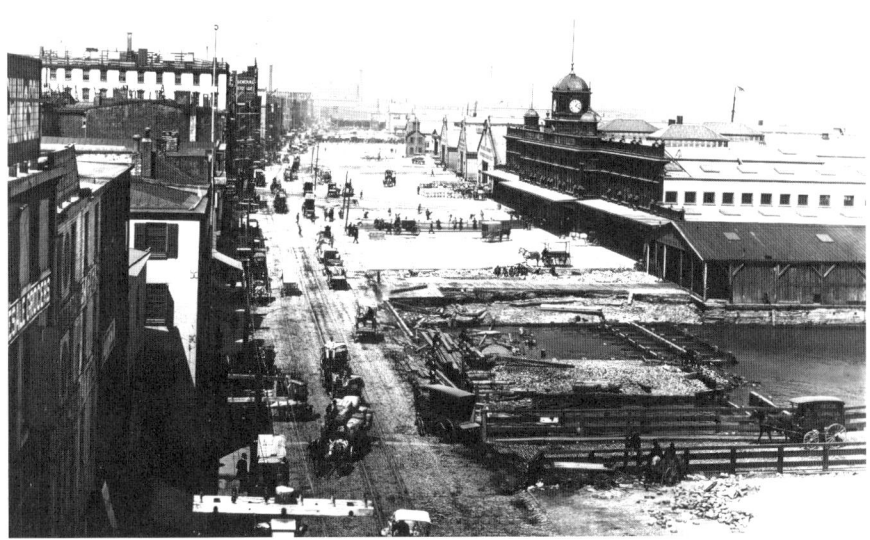

Work is underway in 1899 to widen Delaware Avenue. This view is looking north from Chestnut Street. Notice the Philadelphia Cold Storage Warehouse in the distance—the only building in this image still around. *Philadelphia City Archives.*

bulkhead line basically follows the one that the U.S. secretary of war established on the east side of Delaware Avenue at that time. The line was last modified on September 10, 1940 (33 U.S.C. § 59j).

PAUL BECK'S PLANS FOR THE CENTRAL WATERFRONT

Stephen Girard was not the first to propose bettering Philadelphia's riverfront. In 1820, Paul Beck Jr. (1757–1844) prepared a plan for improving the river's edge between Vine and Spruce Streets. This was the first urban planning exercise in Philadelphia after the laying out of the city itself.

Beck's scheme was for the municipal government to acquire all property from Vine to Spruce Street east of Front Street and then clear away all extant buildings, wharves, streets, steps and so forth. A series of uniform warehouses would be built between Front Street and a wide new avenue by the Delaware. Each warehouse would stand on its own forty- by one-

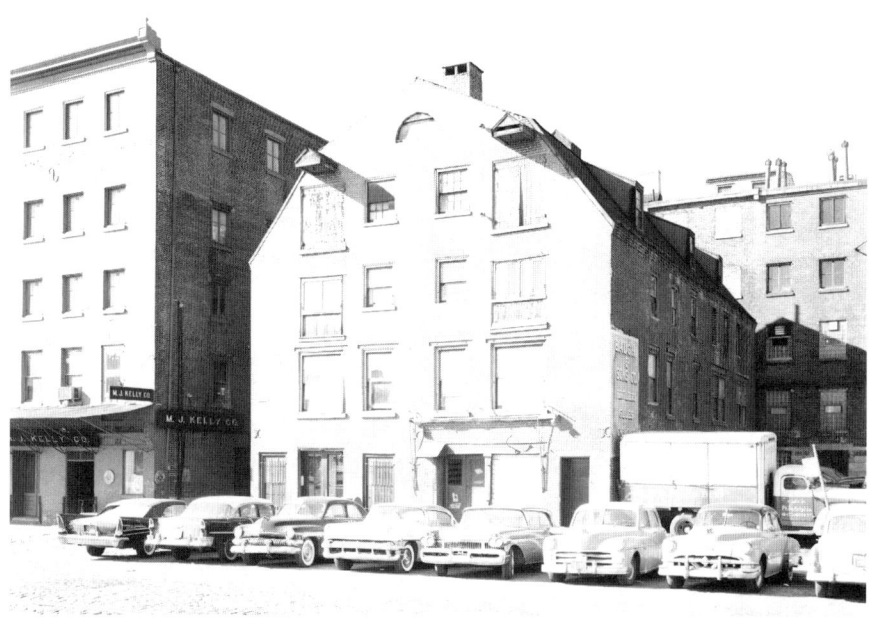

The Beck-Care Warehouse at 18–20 South Delaware Avenue, erected in the late eighteenth century by Paul Beck. From 1860 to 1954, the building was the headquarters of a fertilizer maker. When it was demolished for I-95 in 1967, this was the last surviving eighteenth-century warehouse on the Philadelphia waterfront. *Library of Congress (HABS)*.

Delaware Avenue (Columbus Boulevard)

hundred-foot block, separated by alleys. These improvements were estimated to cost $3,651,000—an astronomical sum back then.

Paul Beck submitted his plan to Stephen Girard for his opinion, but Girard curiously opposed it. Yet it surely must have suggested to Girard that giving Philadelphia money to develop the central Delaware frontage would help the city immensely.

Remarkably similar, Girard and Beck were virtual waterfront successors to Benjamin Franklin and Philip Syng. Like Girard, Paul Beck was an importer/exporter, having acquired a fortune in the wine trade (yet another millionaire by the water). Beck, like Girard, was a port warden of Philadelphia who was intimately familiar with the city waterfront. Beck's "counting house" was at Front and Market, and he owned storehouses along the Delaware. (One located between Market and Chestnut Streets stood until the 1960s.) And like Girard, Beck chose to live and work on Philadelphia's riverfront despite its history of dirtiness and disease, and despite being wealthy enough to live elsewhere.

SMITH'S AND WINDMILL ISLANDS

To accommodate the last round of Delaware Avenue widening, a set of narrow islands in the middle of the Delaware River had to be removed. These isles were opposite Philadelphia's wharves, more or less between Market and South Streets.

The two islands had previously been one long isle called Windmill Island, roughly twenty-five acres in size. This land mass was a type of made-earth—the result of accumulated sand and silt carried downriver by ice and spring floods on the Delaware. Windmill Island was not a fixed place, as it washed away at one end as fast as it grew at another. Its name arose from an octagonal windmill at its northern end, assembled in 1746 by one John Harding.

At various times, it was proposed to bridge the channel and to use Windmill Island as a midway point. These plans were opposed by those who foresaw that the island would have to be dredged away someday.

In 1782, a man named Thomas Wilkinson was hanged for piracy on Windmill Island, leading to fanciful stories that the place was a haven for pirates. Other confirmed pirates were hanged there, so the stories may be true. Early murderers of Philadelphia were also taken to Windmill Island for execution.

The Camden and Philadelphia Ferry had its route between Philadelphia's Walnut Street and Camden's Federal Street. The firm was tired of steaming its ferryboats around the isle since the persistent detour added cost to each ferry trip in terms of time and fuel. So it cut a canal across Windmill Island about 1838. (The DRWC's RiverLink Ferry crosses the channel nowadays exactly where this cut used to be.) The canal in effect created two islands: Windmill Island on the south and Smith's Island, somewhat smaller, on the north.

Smith's Island was named after a John Smith who had owned the northern half of Windmill Island and lived there with his family. Willow trees were planted and flourished on Smith's Island. Then, parks, restaurants, lodges and bathing resorts were constructed on it. Floating baths within the Delaware River had operated there as early as 1826.

In the 1880s, Jacob Ridgway built an amusement park on Smith's Island. (This was likely the same man who owned the Ridgway House Hotel.) Ridgway Park became a popular place for Philadelphians to spend a day of frolicking—"mostly for the lower classes" who lived near the docks, as one author wrote. Hot-air balloon ascensions or tightrope walkers would sometimes entertain visitors. The beer garden at Ridgway Park was especially well patronized. Steam ferries crammed with day-trippers left the Walnut Street Wharf every ten minutes.

Windmill Island, meanwhile, supported a lead works, a dye works and coal boat wharves. A charitable resort for sick and underprivileged children was also there starting in 1877. Chartered boats would pick up kids and their parents from congested Philadelphia neighborhoods all along the Delaware frontage. They were taken to Windmill Island to enjoy a day of recreation, fresh air and free bowls of hot soup with crackers.

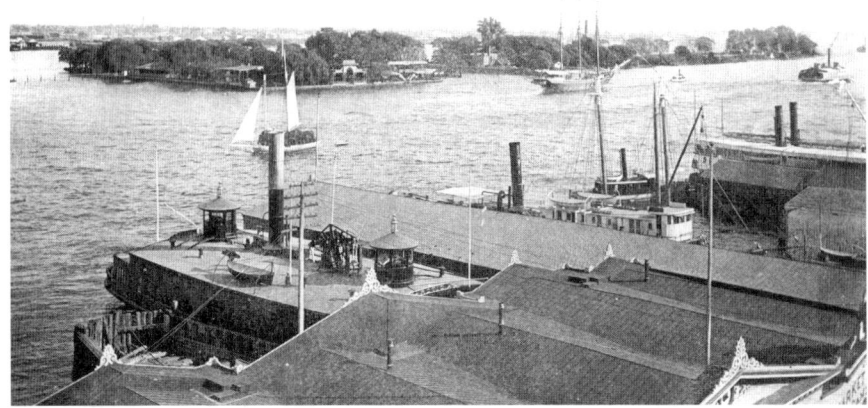

Smith's and Windmill Islands on the Delaware, prior to 1894 and their subsequent removal. *Adam Levine Collection.*

Delaware Avenue (Columbus Boulevard)

The resort, which became nicknamed "Soupy Island," moved to Red Bank, New Jersey, in 1886. The Sanitarium Playground of New Jersey is there to this day, still offering summertime fun—and hot soup—to hundreds of inner-city children of eastern Pennsylvania and southern New Jersey.

The federal government cleared away both Windmill and Smith's Islands in the 1890s. Shipping interests had campaigned to eliminate the landmasses beginning in 1874, calling them impediments to cargo-laden vessels on the river. Plus, the U.S. government wanted a six-hundred-foot-wide shipping channel in the Delaware by then.

Work to remove the islands began in earnest in 1893 and was completed by 1897. The river along the Philadelphia front was also dredged for the first of several times since then. The twenty-six-foot-deep channel was near the center (but closer to Philadelphia) of the pre-existing nineteen-hundred-foot-wide channel between the Philadelphia and Camden pier heads. (The Delaware is much shallower on the Camden side.) The shipping channel is now forty feet deep in the Philadelphia region, but efforts are underway to dredge the river to forty-five feet.

With Windmill and Smith's Islands gone and the channel enlarged as needed, Delaware Avenue could then be made 150 feet wide, and longer replacement docks could be built out into the river as far as 650 feet (but usually not that long). About a dozen new finger piers were built in the ten years following 1897. They were considered vital to Philadelphia's commercial development, since the piers they replaced were too short for vessels being built at that time.

The removal of these islands is an instance of the commercial use of the Delaware taking precedence over preexisting recreational uses. Their elimination to redouble the river's shipping utility presages another mammoth federal transportation–related project about seventy years later: the routing of I-95 through the Philadelphia waterfront. Both projects were the respective superhighways of their day. And fundamentally, they were both implemented to speed commercial traffic through Philadelphia, be it ships and barges or cars and trucks.

THE BELT LINE RAILROAD

Besides providing access to ferries linking Philadelphia to Camden and other New Jersey river towns, Delaware Avenue was the primary transportation corridor for the shipping and handling of food and general cargo for the entire city during the nineteenth and early twentieth centuries. All early photographs of the thoroughfare show a horde of horse-drawn wagons jamming the street. The situation didn't change when motorized trucks took over.

Two sets of railroad tracks ran on Delaware Avenue since the 1890s to meet the freight hauling needs of the docks and industries along the river, with siding tracks connecting to various facilities on both sides of the avenue. Known as the Philadelphia Belt Line Railroad, these tracks ran about eighteen miles from Port Richmond to South Philadelphia.

The Belt Line Railroad was chartered in 1889 and was jointly operated by the three trunk railroads—the Pennsylvania, the Reading and the Baltimore & Ohio—that served Philadelphia during its industrial heyday. The line enabled the efficient moving of merchandise to and from the central waterfront.

Many Philadelphians remember how the Belt Line's tracks and the street's crumbling Belgian-block surface made automobile travel on Delaware Avenue perilous for years and years. Not only that, but wagons and motor vehicles also had to share the jarringly bumpy road with steam locomotives pushing and pulling boxcars.

The Philadelphia Belt Line was never an operating railroad, although it did have track and maintenance equipment and employees. It still exists—chiefly a real estate holding company—and its tracks are still active in South Philadelphia. One set of seldom-used tracks remains in a separate right of way in the middle of Delaware Avenue up to Race Street.

Penn's Landing Trolley

There is talk of using these tracks for a $500 million light-rail line on Delaware Avenue. It would be more for tourists than commuters, but this is nothing new.

From 1982 to 1995, a private group called the Buckingham Valley Trolley Association ran a tourist-oriented trolley service on a one-mile stretch of Belt Line tracks. Volunteers of the Penn's Landing Trolley operated three or four historic trolleys every day during the tourist season. The trolleys ran between the Ben Franklin Bridge and South Philadelphia, making stops at major intersections on Delaware Avenue.

Ridership peaked in 1987. Then, pedestrian ramps over Market, Chestnut and Walnut Streets were completed, diverting foot traffic from Columbus

Delaware Avenue (Columbus Boulevard)

Boulevard (Delaware Avenue). The city government also lost its enthusiasm for trolleys as other activities at Penn's Landing moved to the forefront. The Penn's Landing Trolley shut down in 1995, and the trolley fleet went to the Electric City Trolley Museum in Scranton, Pennsylvania.

"Goodisville"

Delaware Avenue featured many bars for sailors and stevedores in the early years of the 1900s. Some of them were welcoming establishments where men could take a break from manual labor and escape the crowded living conditions of ships and boardinghouses. Others were bawdy places to which sailors would run as soon as they received shore leave.

Some of these taverns doubled as houses of ill repute and contributed to the drunkenness, crime and prostitution that infested sections of the Delaware waterfront. A few bar owners raised fighting dogs and roosters for underground gambling action. As the river was prone to flooding Delaware Avenue, dockworkers could earn free booze by helping bail out saloon cellars. (The Delaware still floods the street now and then.)

It was in this seedy port district that 1950s and '60s paperback author David Goodis (1917–1967) set most of his bleak crime novels. In the essay "David Goodis's Hardboiled Philadelphia," cultural historian Jay Gertzman gave a name to the grimy old waterfront: "Goodisville." It was a tired industrial area of broken paving stones and worn railroad tracks, populated by flophouses, taverns and diners amid decaying warehouses and piers. Philadelphia's Tenderloin (Skid Row) was to the immediate east, above and including the Old City and Callowhill neighborhoods.

The demise of Goodisville, for good or bad, took about twenty years, beginning in the late 1950s. Southwark was cleared for the Interstate, Society Hill was redeveloped and the once-thriving but then-dying central waterfront was remade as Penn's Landing. Urban pioneers, restaurateurs and night clubbers arrived. Hardworking Delaware Avenue became haughty Columbus Boulevard. By the 1980s, Goodisville was finished.

Even so, a 1990 *Philadelphia Inquirer* editorial on Delaware Avenue declared, "The roadway is so damn ugly, decrepit and dangerous no one would want to be anywhere near it."

Delaware Avenue versus Columbus Boulevard

In 1992, the Italian community of South Philadelphia persuaded Philadelphia City Council to celebrate the 500th anniversary of Christopher Columbus sailing to America by renaming Delaware Avenue after the explorer. Citizens in the northern precincts of the city, aided by members of the local Lenni-Lenape tribe, fought the name change. A compromise was reached in which the avenue was renamed only south of Spring Garden Street. Nevertheless, street signs reading "C Columbus Blvd" were defaced for years after.

Christopher Columbus did get something else: the *Columbus Monument* at Penn's Landing, facing Dock Street. This three-sided stainless steel obelisk commemorates Columbus's 1492 voyage and the role that immigrants have played in developing Philadelphia and the United States. Designed by world-renowned architect Robert Venturi, the Columbus Monument was installed in 1992 and rises 106 feet.

The Commonwealth of Pennsylvania paved and landscaped Delaware Avenue in the 1990s. Instead of a rough stone roadway filled with ruts, rats and railroad tracks, the street is now smooth, well lit and ornamented with greenery. Columbus Boulevard is, indeed, a fulfillment of Stephen Girard's desire for a wide, tree-lined thoroughfare along the Delaware.

The Port of Philadelphia Today

The tough longshoremen of Goodisville were mostly a memory by the 1970s, as containerization and highway-based shipping had made the original Philadelphia port obsolete. The city's cargo-handling operations by then had moved to more spacious port facilities along the Delaware River.

Most Philadelphia-bound cargo ships dock primarily at the quay-type piers at the 112-acre Packer Avenue Marine Terminal south of Snyder Avenue in South Philadelphia. Others head to the 116-acre Tioga Marine Terminal far north of the city's original waterfront. Both of these facilities were built in the 1970s by the Philadelphia Port Corporation, a nonprofit, quasi-public port agency established in 1965 to replace the Department of Wharves, Docks and Ferries.

Just a handful of workers are needed at these terminals to operate overhead cranes that unload containers stuffed with cargo from around the world. (These massive gantry cranes are a bit more powerful than the "fine

Delaware Avenue (Columbus Boulevard)

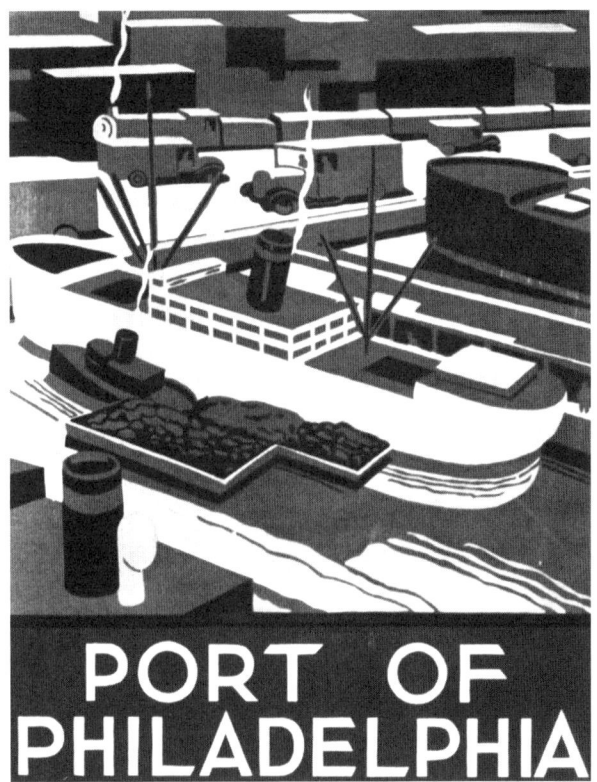

A 1930s WPA poster.
Library of Congress.

necessary Crane" on Samuel Carpenter's Wharf.) All this goes on behind barbed wire and chain-link fences. This is a far cry from when visitors would drop by Joshua Humphreys' shipyard for a firsthand look at naval vessels being constructed or when prostitutes used to prowl the busy docks and markets along the Delaware.

These days, the Port of Philadelphia is among the largest freshwater ports in the world and one of the most active in the United States. It's the largest port of entry for produce in the United States and the nation's chief break-bulk port. It is also the fourth-largest port for processing imported goods in the country and the only American port serviced by three railroads. And Interstate 95 is, of course, nearby.

The Philadelphia Regional Port Authority, created in 1990 as an independent agency of the Commonwealth of Pennsylvania, manages Philadelphia's cargo piers and terminals today. The authority's mission statement includes this: "Nothing is more important than protecting the Port of Philadelphia's 300-plus year legacy as a major center of maritime industrial commerce."

19

Penn's Landing

Festivities and Tragedies on the Water

Penn's Landing is so named, obviously, because of its proximity to where William Penn first entered the future city of Philadelphia and to honor this event.

Genesis of the Modern Waterfront

The old cargo and passenger piers along Delaware Avenue had become decrepit by the mid-twentieth century. Only six of the twenty-three piers along the waterfront were still in use for waterborne commerce by 1956. Once the foundation of Philadelphia's commercial development and strength, the downtown docks had become outmoded and a blight to the city. Some of the old piers, vacated one by one, suffered fires that destroyed them. Others, mainly those between Market and South Streets, were removed or filled in to create the recreational area known as Penn's Landing.

The germ of Penn's Landing can be traced back to December 1947. This is when the Philadelphia City Planning Commission released its *Preliminary Plan for Old City Area*. An illustration showed a marina between Chestnut and Spruce Streets, a large wholesale center surrounding a waterfront park between Market and Chestnut Streets, and an expressway taking the place of Delaware Avenue.

Then, in late 1951, Thomas Brown, director of the Department of Wharves, Docks and Ferries, proposed creating a "small and attractive

Penn's Landing

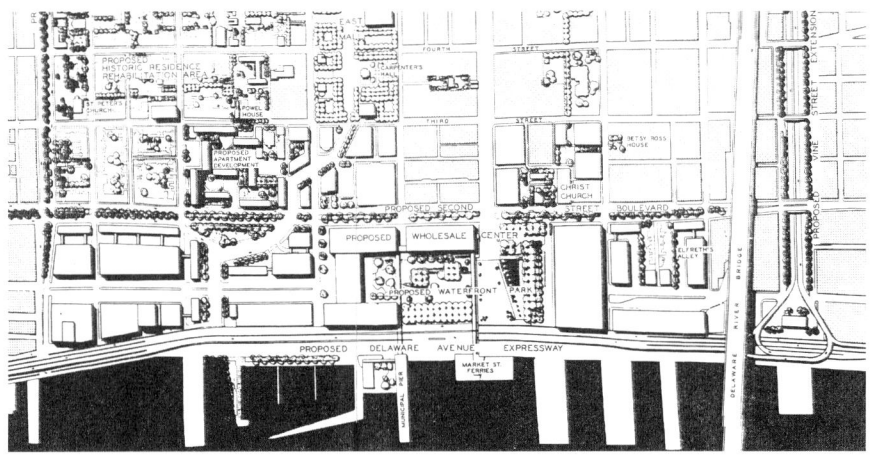

The first incarnation of Penn's Landing. *From the Philadelphia City Planning Commission's 1947 Preliminary Plan for Old City Area.*

yacht basin and a large recreation pier which visitors will remember" on the site of the derelict piers then between Market and Chestnut Streets. Brown observed that the condition of these docks—most owned by the Pennsylvania Railroad—did "nothing to enhance the appearance of [the] waterfront." The modest plan was contingent on the railroad abandoning its ferry and freight operations in that area, which it did in 1952.

However, Penn's Landing as it ultimately became, was envisioned in the 1950s and '60s by Edmund Bacon (1910–2005), head planner and executive director at the Philadelphia Planning Commission from 1949 to 1970. He based his plan on the 1947 *Preliminary Plan* and his underlying conviction that publicly financed improvements would stimulate private investment in Philadelphia's downtown waterfront.

The architectural firm Geddes Brecher Qualls Cunningham issued the first true master plan for Penn's Landing in 1963 on behalf of the Planning Commission. The prologue of *Penn's Landing: A Master Plan for Philadelphia's Downtown Waterfront* states:

> *The City of Philadelphia has acquired the waterfront properties in this nautical mile and has prepared a comprehensive master plan designed to realize its full historic, aesthetic and commercial potential. A careful balance will be maintained between public and private investment throughout the two main stages of construction—so that the direct income from privately financed elements and indirect (tax-generated) income from publicly financed*

PHILADELPHIA'S LOST WATERFRONT

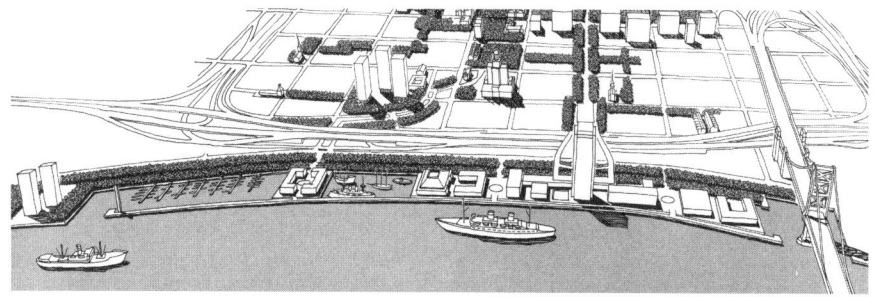

An early drawing of Penn's Landing. Note the unbuilt Crosstown Expressway (I-695) on the left. Note also the mirror image of Penn's Landing as planned—only the southern portion was built. *From* Penn's Landing: A Master Plan *(1963).*

elements will support the high standards of design and operation essential at this key location.

The plan included a recreational wharf at Dock Street, a boat basin, a maritime museum and a "Port Tower" at the base of Market Street. To put this all into effect, Mayor James Tate, in 1970, set up the Penn's Landing Corporation as a subsidiary of the Old Philadelphia Development Corporation.

CONSTRUCTION BEGINS!

The first of the rotting ferry landings and wharves to be demolished in the late 1950s were those of the Pennsylvania Railroad. Actual construction of Penn's Landing began in 1967. The segment between Market and South Streets was constructed on landfill (made-earth) in preparation for the U.S. Bicentennial. This first phase of the project consisted of a marina and a protective breakwater with a promenade on top.

Penn's Landing was designed to mirror itself: a comparable breakwater and marina were to be built north of Market Street. If this phase of the project had been completed, Piers 3 and 5 would have been demolished, as would Piers 9 and 11. But only half of Penn's Landing was finished due to the lack of both public funds and private investment. There's certainly no intention of ever carrying out the full design, especially with the condo communities of Piers 3 and 5 in the way.

The rough-and-tumble dock area along Delaware Avenue was slowly transformed into an appealing place for Philadelphians and tourists to

Penn's Landing

pursue leisure activities as Penn's Landing evolved into Philadelphia's premier multi-use riverside park. At the same time, sailboats and cruise ships supplanted tugboats and cargo ships in plying the Delaware.

In the 1980s, the City of Philadelphia built the Great Plaza at Penn's Landing, a public amphitheater at the bottom of Chestnut Street. Together, it and Festival Pier at Spring Garden Street provide a venue for various free and fee-based festivals, performances and other events. Fireworks are routinely presented on the Delaware, and a seasonal ice-skating rink, the Blue Cross RiverRink, is often jam-packed. What's more, the Penn's Landing Marina supports kayak and swan boat rentals. All these activities on the Philadelphia waterfront would have been deemed preposterous as recently as 1970.

The periodic pyrotechnics at Penn's Landing bring to mind the fireworks display that Captain John André organized in 1778 for the Mischianza. Plus, the outdoor skating rink is reminiscent of the era when ice skaters twirled atop the frozen Delaware.

Failures to Launch

Enhancements to Penn's Landing have been planned for decades, but all have been shelved for one reason or another. The first proposal was in 1973 for a complex of office and apartment towers. Several grandiose schemes have been offered and withdrawn since then. The most recent serious plan, a $200 million Family Entertainment Center, would have had retail shops, restaurants, a three-thousand-seat amphitheater, two ice-skating rinks and a fifteen-screen movie theater. Proposed by Simon DeBartolo Group, it was dropped in 2002 after five years of talk.

The canyon of Interstate 95 paralleling Penn's Landing is what has doomed all of this possible redevelopment. The Delaware Expressway will continue to stifle the central waterfront of Philadelphia for a very long time. With its six lanes of traffic and Belt Line tracks, Columbus Boulevard does not help matters.

A bridge at Market Street helps provide access to the Delaware River from Old City Philadelphia. This high viaduct crosses over both I-95 and Columbus Boulevard and then loops to Chestnut Street. Its excessive height was dictated by the need to clear the partially elevated highway. Two ungainly vehicular ramps (the "scissor ramps") lead from Columbus Boulevard up to Market Street and from Chestnut Street down to Columbus Boulevard.

A drab flight of concrete steps at the end of Market Street connects the viaduct to the waterfront's lower level, providing pedestrians a way to get to Penn's Landing. This tall, spindly stairway can be deemed a contemporary successor to the bank steps of William Penn.

Penn Praxis's thirty-year plan for the Philadelphia riverfront calls for all parking lots and other unsightly hardscape at Penn's Landing to be turned into green space. Whether any of this will ever happen is uncertain.

The Skylink Aerial Tram and the "Keystone State Arch"

The strange concrete arch by the river between Market and Chestnut Streets is the tower support for the Skylink Aerial Tram, a never-completed ski lift–type ride to Camden. Gondolas were intended to have whisked as many as two thousand people an hour across the river at this point.

The Delaware River Port Authority spent some $13 million building the tower structure and its counterpart in Camden before work ceased in 2003. Controversy had erupted over whether the Skylink was a transit project or a tourist attraction and whether toll money from local Delaware River crossings should be used to construct it. The tram's tower support was left standing in the wake as a stark example of conflict relating to activity by the water and the riverfront's overall use and enjoyment.

A recent proposal is to make the π-shaped support a state memorial to commemorate Pennsylvania's founding not far from that locale. The monolithic structure would be named the Keystone State Arch.

The Irish Memorial

A proper memorial is already located at Front and Chestnut Streets: the Irish Memorial. This striking bronze sculpture-in-the round brings to life the story of An Gorta Mór (the Great Hunger) and pays respect to the Irish men, women and children who perished during the famine between 1845 and 1850 caused by potato blight. It also celebrates the millions of Irish immigrants who came to the United States seeking a better life. Crafted by eminent sculptor Glenna Goodacre, the work was dedicated on October 25, 2003.

The 1.75-acre memorial grounds are on top of one of the covers above Interstate 95. This high vantage point overlooks the Delaware River and is a

Penn's Landing

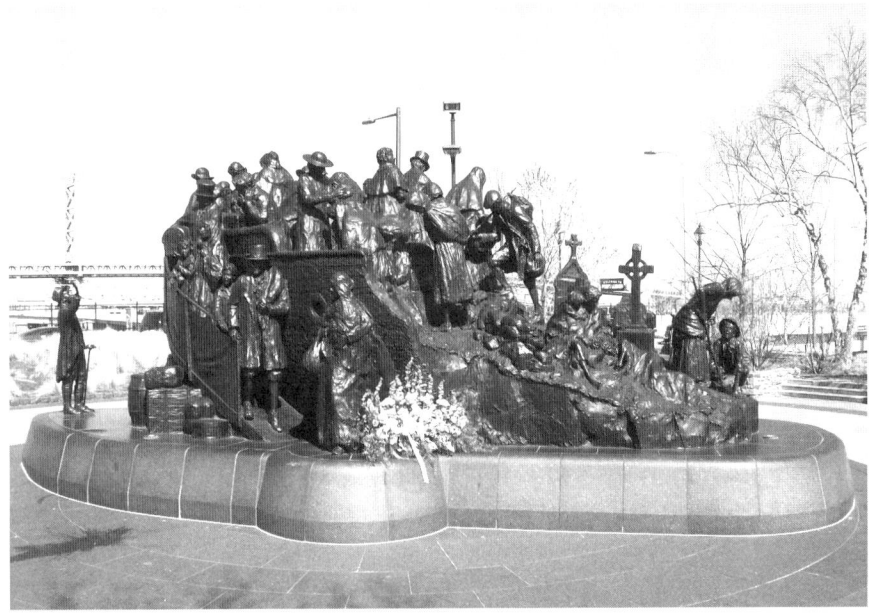

The Irish Memorial, installed in 2003 at Front and Chestnut Streets on one of the two covers atop I-95. *Photo by the author.*

fitting location for the monument because countless Irish disembarked ships and entered Philadelphia (and the nation) along the riverfront on either side of that location. Unfortunately, as with Foglietta Plaza and the Vietnam Veterans Memorial, the ever-present sound of vehicles on I-95 ruins what is meant to be a contemplative place.

INDEPENDENCE SEAPORT MUSEUM

Independence Seaport Museum (ISP) at Penn's Landing explores the role that the Port of Philadelphia has played regionally and nationally in trade, immigration, defense and recreation. It features interactive exhibits and over ten thousand maritime artifacts, including navigational instruments, naval uniforms and model ships.

State-of-the-art exhibits make this museum the preeminent facility for preserving and sharing the maritime tradition of the Delaware River and Bay. The centerpiece attraction, Home Port: Philadelphia, explores the city's waterfront activities over time. Immigrant stories are shared at a re-creation of the Washington Avenue Immigration Station. A Navy Yard exhibit highlights the life of a longshoreman. The Workshop on the Water shows the skills and heritage of wooden boat building and sailing on the Delaware.

The Historic Ship Zone includes the USS *Becuna* (SS-319), a World War II submarine that gives visitors the chance to glimpse the lives of members of the nation's "silent service." Few World War II subs are on display in America, and this is one of them. The Balao-cless vessel was commissioned in May 1944 as the submarine flagship of the Southwest Pacific Fleet under General Douglas MacArthur. Very active during the war, the *Becuna* was awarded four Battle Stars and a Presidential Unit Citation for its efforts.

ISP's true star, however, is—or was—the naval cruiser USS *Olympia*. A National Historic Landmark, the *Olympia* was Admiral George Dewey's flagship in the Spanish-American War and is the sole surviving ship from that contest. After decommissioning in the early 1920s, the *Olympia* went to the Philadelphia Naval Yard, where it stayed for over thirty years before the Cruiser Olympia Association moved it to the foot of Race Street in 1958. It opened there as a museum before being moved to Penn's Landing. As of 2011, the vessel's fate is in jeopardy: the *Olympia* is set to be disposed of because its hull is rusting badly.

It's too bad that Philadelphia has lost its shipbuilding and repair expertise. Any one of several regional shipyards in operation decades ago could have restored the *Olympia*, the Philadelphia Navy Yard being the likeliest. But sadly, even that facility closed in 1996. (A small commercial shipyard is, however, now operating at the Navy Yard site.)

Independence Seaport Museum is housed in the old Port of History Museum building, built by the Commonwealth of Pennsylvania for the U.S. Bicentennial. Finished a bit late in 1977, the edifice had a rocky financial and political start and sat empty for years. The "white elephant" on the riverbank was taken over by the Philadelphia Maritime Museum, which changed its name when the place reopened in 1995.

GAZELA AND *JUPITER*

Penn's Landing is homeport to the *Gazela*, the world's oldest and largest wooden square-rigged barkentine still sailing. Dating back to 1883, the vessel is owned and operated by the Philadelphia Ship Preservation Guild. The Philadelphia Maritime Museum brought it to Philadelphia in 1971 to represent the city in the U.S. Bicentennial's Tall Ships Parade in New York Harbor. The *Gazela* has been promoting the City of Brotherly Love ever

Penn's Landing

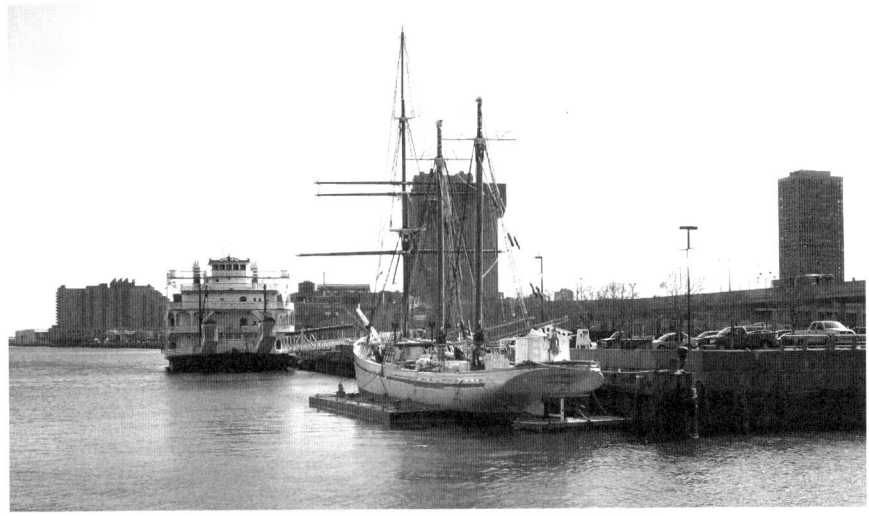

The *Gazela* and *Philadelphia Belle* docked at Penn's Landing, an area once filled with piers. *Right*: One of the Society Hill Towers. *Distant left*: the Dockside condominium. *Center*: The Independence Seaport Museum and the Skylink Aerial Tram's tower support (behind the *Gazela*).

since, sailing to ports around the nation and the world. In this way, the ship acts as Philadelphia's goodwill ambassador and carries on the city's long maritime tradition.

The Ship Preservation Guild also owns and operates the tugboat *Jupiter*. Built in 1902 at the Philadelphia shipyard of Neafie & Levy, this is the oldest continually operating tug on the Delaware River. The tug was bought by the Independent Pier Company of Philadelphia in 1939 after having worked in New York Harbor as the *Sacony #14*. Renamed *Jupiter*, it helped launch naval vessels from shipyards on the Delaware during the Second World War and continued working commercially until the Guild acquired it in 1989.

The *Jupiter* is still a functioning tug but it also participates in educational programs, festivals and even boat parades. The occasional flotillas on the Delaware are not all that different from the procession of bedecked barges that transported guests to the Mischianza in 1778.

Moshulu

Another exceptional ship at Penn's Landing is the *Moshulu*, a 394-foot steel clipper that is the world's oldest and largest four-masted sailing ship. This vessel's story is too convoluted to summarize here, but a short account of its tumultuous time in Philadelphia is in order.

The *Moshulu* was purchased for use as a floating restaurant in the 1970s. It was towed across the Atlantic first to New York City and then to Philadelphia. While serving as an exotic eatery at Penn's Landing, a four-alarm fire broke out in the galley in 1989. Fire and smoke/water damage closed the restaurant for years. While the *Moshulu* languished, it was vandalized and stripped of much of its gear. But in 1995, the ship was purchased by H.M.S. Ventures and underwent an $11 million restoration.

Misfortune struck again in 2000 when Pier 34 South—where the *Moshulu* was then docked—collapsed into the Delaware River. The ship closed at that point. Two years later, it was moved to the Penn's Landing Marina and shortly reopened as a South Seas restaurant.

Tragedy on the Water: Pier 34 South, Ride the Ducks and the Ferryboat *New Jersey*

The collapse of Pier 34 occurred in the evening of May 18, 2000. The far section of the pier suddenly fell into the Delaware, killing three women and injuring dozens others. They were all partying at Club Heat, an outdoor nightclub at the end of the dock, then called Eli's Pier 34. Darkness, debris and river currents hampered rescue efforts, as did the threat of the rest of the pier's collapse.

The owner of Pier 34 and the manager of the club were ultimately charged for failure to maintain and repair the wharf's foundation, even after weeks of visible warnings that the deck was shifting. They both pleaded guilty and were sentenced to community service and a year of house arrest. The Reading Railroad had built the pier in 1909 for use in loading coal onto ships.

A more recent calamity on the Delaware River occurred on July 7, 2010, when a disabled Ride the Ducks sightseeing boat was run over by a sludge barge pushed by a tugboat with an inattentive crew. About forty tourists went into the river when the amphibious vehicle sank. Many of these people, including two who died, were Hungarians visiting the United States as part of a missionary exchange program.

First responders included men and equipment from the Coast Guard Station at Washington Avenue. The accident's location was at the foot of Chestnut Street, a stone's throw from the Great Plaza at Penn's Landing and at a spot once occupied by Smith's Island. The Georgia-based Ducks company had operated on the Delaware without incident since 2003.

Penn's Landing

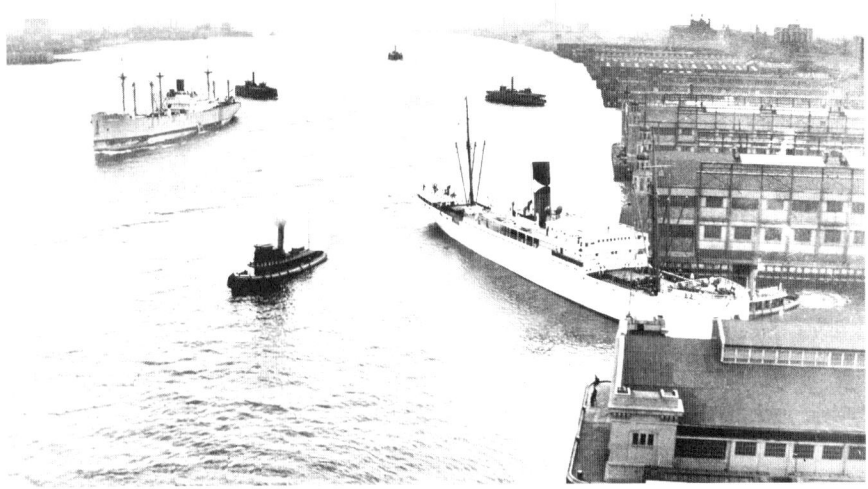

The Delaware has always been a working river, as this early to mid-twentieth-century photo indicates. Piers 3 and 5 North are at the center of a line of a dozen or so finger piers. Penn's Landing was later built in place of most of these piers. *Philadelphia City Archives.*

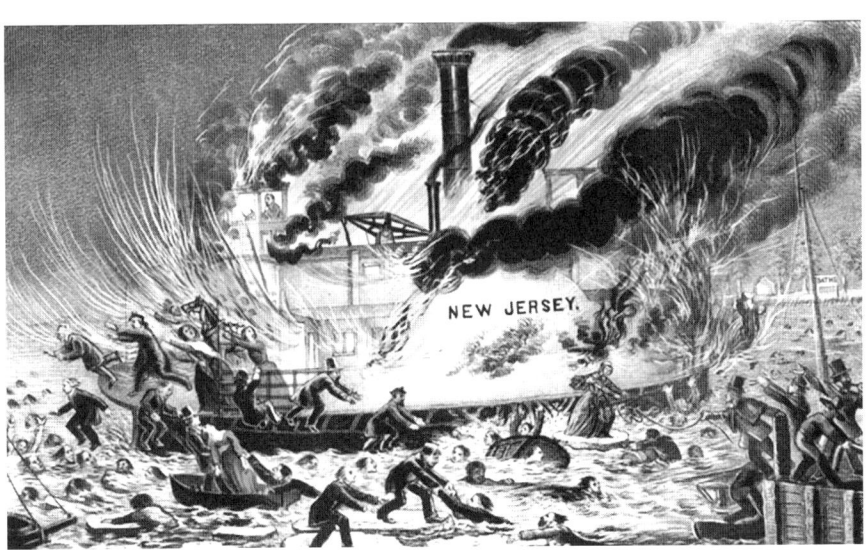

Another exciting print: "Terrible Conflagration and Destruction of the Steam-Boat ferry *New Jersey*." *The Library Company of Philadelphia.*

Both of these tragedies underscore the growing tension between various activities on the river. The Delaware is a working waterway. Its use as such has diminished since the 1950s, but there's no question that sizable ships and barges still ply the waterway daily. On the other hand, its use for recreational purposes has grown dramatically in recent times, with a huge increase of sailboats, speedboats, jet skis and tourist crafts since the 1980s, as well as dockside clubs and the like.

Then again, any activity on the water is inherently dangerous. Take, for instance, the disaster of March 15, 1856, when the steam ferry *New Jersey* caught fire in the middle of the ice-filled Delaware. Operated by the Philadelphia and Camden Ferry Company, the ferryboat was carrying almost one hundred passengers, mostly New Jerseyans. It left the Walnut Street Wharf at 8:00 p.m. and was headed for Camden via the canal between Smith's and Windmill Islands.

Approaching the canal, the boat's smokestack was discovered to be on fire. The captain turned the boat around and steamed north with the tide toward the Arch Street Wharf. But before the *New Jersey* could be made fast, the engine room and pilothouse burst into flames. Now without power and out of control, the ferry was pushed by ice floes to the middle of the river. Passengers tried to save themselves by jumping onto icebergs or into the frigid water. The *New Jersey* finally went under just off the Camden shore. Sixty-one men and women drowned or burned to death on the icy Delaware.

The Residences at Dockside and Waterfront Square

Immediately north of Pier 34 is a condominium complex called the Residences at Dockside. This sixteen-story edifice was constructed atop the remains of Pier 30 South, once known as the Kenilworth Street Pier. The high-rise broke ground in 2000 and later opened as a rental community with 242 apartments. It went condo in 2006. As with Piers 3 and 5, the Delaware River flows underneath the ocean liner–shaped structure. Dockside is just one indication of the renewed appeal of living on Philadelphia's riverfront.

The most conspicuous indication is Waterfront Square Condominium, a three-tower multiplex just north of Spring Garden Street. This development is slated to have five buildings ranging from twenty-two

Penn's Landing

to thirty-five stories with a total of 780 condominiums. That such a large, towering housing development should occupy this site would have dumbfounded Philadelphians a half century ago. The Waterfront Square compound totals ten acres, all of it made-earth.

Gambling on the Delaware

SugarHouse Casino is directly north of Waterfront Square. Philadelphia became the largest city in the United States to host a gambling casino when this venue opened for business on September 23, 2010. Lawsuits filed by neighborhood protesters and others delayed the opening for years. This was the strongest and most recent instance of conflict on the Delaware—other than the ongoing debate about river dredging.

SugarHouse gets its name from the Pennsylvania Sugar Refinery Company, situated on that property from 1881 to 1984 and employing over fifteen hundred men and women during World War II. The $355 million casino has brought attention to the potential of other development along Delaware Avenue in that section of town. Another casino was planned for the river's edge in South Philadelphia, but that project ran into difficulties.

The public clamor concerning SugarHouse disregarded the long history of gambling on the west bank of the Delaware going back to William Penn's era. When Quakers dwelled in riverbank caves, gambling went hand in hand with prostitution along the waterway. Betting occurred wherever sailors and pirates gathered to eat and drink, and tavern owners operated games of chance in their back rooms to meet the demand. This was happening well into the twentieth century.

Riverboat gambling had been proposed for the Delaware in the 1990s before standalone casinos were considered. But there was surely much gambling on the river for centuries.

20
THE DELAWARE EXPRESSWAY (I-95)

VOILÀ—A SUPERHIGHWAY IN THE MIDST

[The] *deviation from* [William Penn's] *original plan* [for the Philadelphia waterfront] *is much to be regretted, as had that been adhered to, a pleasing view of the Delaware from Front street would have been obtained, and thus have not only added greatly to the beauty of the city, but have admitted a refreshing body of air from the river, and prevented the accumulation of filth, which, to the great injury of the inhabitants, has, and ever will be the consequence of the erection of dwellings in such confined situations.*

These words appear in *The Picture of Philadelphia* (1811) by Dr. James Mease (1771–1846). A local historian of the early 1800s, he lived and worked on the west side of Front Street next to Pine, so he must have known the story of William Penn's plans for the Delaware waterfront.

Maybe Dr. Mease wrote the anonymous piece about the embankment steps that appeared in the June 24, 1824 issue of the *Aesculapian Register*:

> *We are requested to ask whoever it may concern, by what authority the* public *stairs, running from Front to Water Street, are in several places shut up—and have been so for a great length of time. It was very proper during the yellow fever; but what has called for its continuance? If this is not soon obviated, what is* public *property will probably soon be claimed as private. It is highly probable that by some* entering wedge *like the present, the citizens have been deprived of that beautiful esplanade and fine prospect, which William Penn contemplated in the original plan of Philadelphia.*

The Delaware Expressway (I-95)

A few of Penn's stairwells were thus blocked off during the Philadelphia's yellow fever contagions of the 1790s. They apparently remained closed for some time after, and this became a matter of public alarm. Some of the stairs were annexed by adjacent property owners, as the writer had foreseen.

But what the writer could not have foreseen was the heavy-handed threading of Interstate 95 through the city's waterfront. The Delaware Expressway has forever deprived citizens of the "beautiful esplanade and fine prospect, which William Penn contemplated in the original plan of Philadelphia"—more than the construction of wharves and whatnot on the east side of Front Street ever did, let alone the closing or elimination of a few public stairways.

Origins of I-95

An elevated thoroughfare through Philadelphia's river district had been planned since 1932, when the Regional Planning Federation—predecessor agency to the Delaware Valley Regional Planning Commission—proposed a limited-access highway along the Delaware as part of a citywide parkway system. Plans languished until 1937, when a new proposal was issued, this time for an industrial highway dubbed the "Delaware Skyway" that would be built on top of Delaware Avenue.

Nothing happened until after World War II when engineers of the Pennsylvania Department of Highways reexamined the old plans and approved a route for the Delaware Expressway as part of the anticipated Interstate highway network. By 1955, a new plan called for a six-lane elevated artery through downtown Philadelphia alongside the Delaware River. It was revised again as an eight-lane arterial Interstate in 1959.

The Department of Highways started construction of the Philadelphia stretch that year under the Federal Aid Highway Act of 1956, but it was not until the late 1960s that the highway started to tear a path through the city's central waterfront. The recently established Independence National Historic Park fixed the roadway's location on the west and Delaware Avenue set its location on the east.

The Delaware Expressway was pursued with urban renewal in mind, too. Deserted and expendable warehouses and industrial sites were to be removed for both the highway and Penn's Landing.

What's This About a Highway Along the Delaware?

Citizens and members of the Philadelphia City Council raised concerns with state and federal officials about the highway's location in the early 1960s. To assuage growing unease, the Department of Highways displayed a scale model of the road's downtown portion at Wanamaker's Department Store in 1963–64. The mock-up depicted an elevated expressway hugging the west bank of the Delaware and supported mostly with earth fill.

Upon seeing the model, architect Frank Weise (1918–2003) confronted Edmund Bacon. He warned the city planner that the freeway would cut off Center City from its historic waterfront and would doom the city's goal of populating the river's edge with housing, parks and shops.

Bacon was unwilling to intercede, telling Weise that he was not "living in the age of the automobile." So the architect-turned-civic-activist organized a team of independent designers to develop an alternative scheme. This group, the Philadelphia Architects Committee, proposed an expressway that was both depressed and covered.

Meanwhile, increased public distress helped form the Committee to Preserve Philadelphia's Historic Gateway, chaired by attorney Stanhope Browne. This group looked to waterfront sites throughout the world for inspiration.

The two committees hired an engineering firm to evaluate the feasibility and cost of the substitute design. The resulting report was published as *The Proposal for a Covered Below-Grade Expressway Through Philadelphia's Historic Riverfront* (1965). This study reveals a colossal problem that engineers had to resolve in building the highway so close to the Delaware:

> *Because the Expressway is to be built near the Delaware River, water from that river would exert an upward thrust on the Expressway, which would in effect be floating in silt. To counteract this hydrostatic pressure, the* [Pennsylvania] *Department* [of Highways] *proposes to place the highway upon a concrete mat which in some places would be about 14 feet thick; the weight of the mat would be used to hold down the Expressway. The maximum depth of construction would be 37 feet below the 100-year high water level of the Delaware River.*

Builders of the Delaware Avenue Elevated had avoided this problem by constructing an elevated line rather than continuing the Market Street Subway through a city block of somewhat unstable made-earth to Delaware Avenue, which itself rests on made-earth.

The Delaware Expressway (I-95)

Furthermore, the report considered and foretold the issues that became so clear after Highway 95 was completed:

If the current Department proposal is chosen, a trench containing ten lanes of traffic would become a dominant feature of the area, totally alien to its historic character. The old city would be forever separated from the riverfront where it originated. The Committee design, on the other hand, hides the massive scale of the expressway facility and prevents the ten lanes of automobile, bus and truck traffic from destroying the intimate living relation which Philadelphia's historic buildings have with each other and with the river.

Separate from the visual obstructions created by the Department proposal would be the visual distraction which the open trench and ten lanes of traffic would create in an area characterized by historic buildings and streets, all constructed in a uniformly small scale. In this architectural context an exposed expressway would appear as a totally alien intrusion, hopelessly in conflict with its surrounding. The view of the many thousands of persons who annually stand at the foot of the slight hill leading down through the historical park would appear to be dominated almost exclusively by the massive highway, rather than by Penn's Landing and the river.

An open Expressway in a trench, as the Planning Commission recognized, tends permanently to divide and differentiate the areas through which it runs.

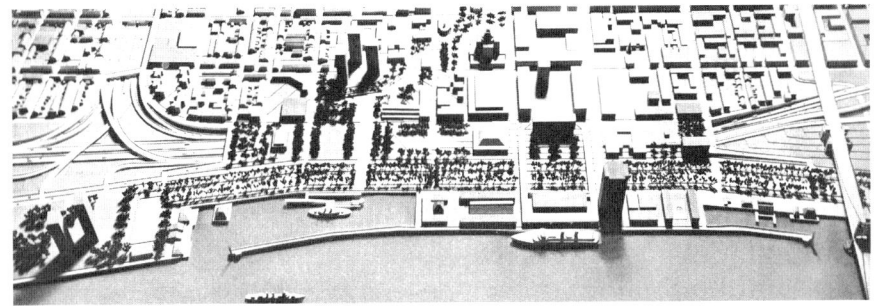

A model of the central waterfront showing "15 key acres recovered for Philadelphia" if I-95 was covered according to the proposals of the committees that sought to mitigate the highway's effects through Penn's Landing. *From* The Proposal for a Covered Below-Grade Expressway Through Philadelphia's Historic Riverfront *(1965).*

The effect of this division would be to place Penn's Landing on the "wrong" side of the Expressway and convert that project into an isolated stepchild of Philadelphia's renaissance. The open Expressway would have other, non-visual effects. For example, it would do little to limit the sound of the thousands of cars, trucks and buses which will be using the Expressway each day.

Despite this, the Philadelphia Architects Committee and the Committee to Preserve Philadelphia's Historic Gateway did not seek to stop the highway, nor did the groups call for its rerouting. The "you can't fight city hall" mentality had evidently worn down the opposition.

Besides, many Philadelphians (and others) wanted I-95 to be built through Philadelphia so that the city could benefit from being right on part of the new Interstate Highway System. The impression was that the freeway would effectively serve the same purpose for travelers as the Kingshighway did some three hundred years before. But the King's Highway, I-95 is not.

Alternatives, Tunnels and Lids, Oh My!

The 1965 proposal offered an alternate design that would have placed a concrete top over the highway from Arch to Pine Streets. Buildings and parks were to be built above this lid, which would be overlaid with earth fill and would thus be heavy enough to prevent the river from pushing up the road deck. The concrete mat's thickness could then be reduced to less than fourteen feet, which would then allow the roadway to be lowered an additional ten feet. As such, all major east–west streets from Race to Pine could continue to Delaware Avenue via overpasses.

Prodded by the proposal, state officials produced plans for an eight-lane expressway sunk below the level of Front Street, along with a deck over the highway from Arch to Pine. Vice President Hubert Humphrey formed a multidisciplinary committee in 1967 to assess the design. This group ordered the federal government to accept a below-grade design, but only from Market to Lombard. It rejected the six-block cover because of the extra expense of building and ventilating such a long tunnel. The cost was estimated to be $25,235,500 more than the Pennsylvania Department of Highways' initial plan.

The state and federal governments eventually (grudgingly) built lids over two short segments of the freeway: Chestnut to Sansom and Dock to Delancey. These concrete decks produce two tunnels totaling one thousand feet. Fifteen

The Delaware Expressway (I-95)

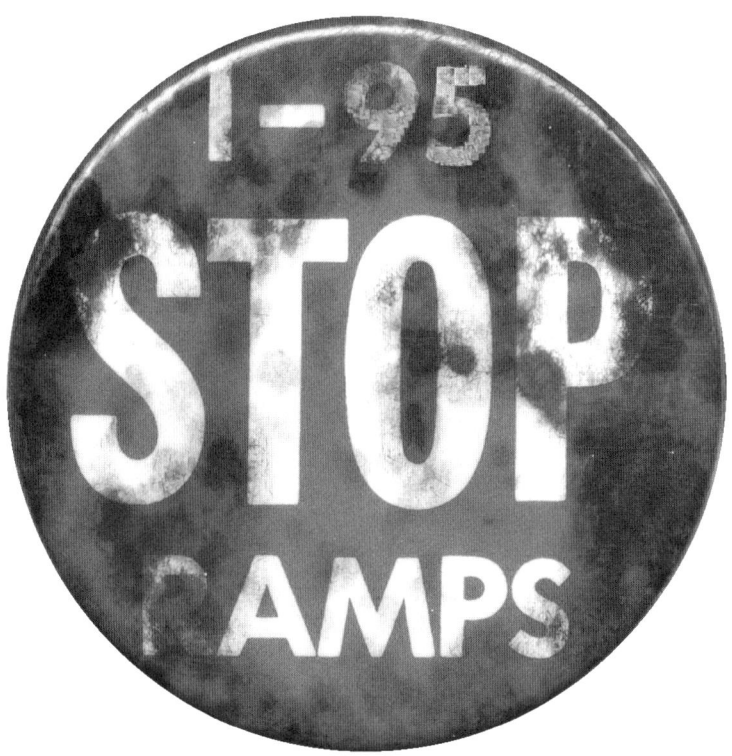

A well-worn "Stop I-95 Ramps" button. *Photo courtesy of Rob Kettell, an Elfreth's Alley resident who was involved in preventing highway ramps from tearing down the alley's eastern portion.*

lanes of traffic—for mainline I-95, entrance ramps and shoulders—pass through them. The Pennsylvania Department of Transportation designed the retaining walls between these sections with the view that a middle cover would be added later. This has not happened. Foglietta Plaza is on the longer southern cover.

The wall supporting the deck between Chestnut and Walnut Streets is noticeably high alongside Columbus Boulevard. This is precisely where Philadelphia's first wharf—Samuel Carpenter's, with its "fine necessary Crane"—was located long ago. The expressway then presents a sheer wall north of Chestnut Street as it rises to become an elevated structure by Race Street.

A New Noisy Neighbor by the River

The Center City section of I-95 opened over Labor Day weekend in 1979. The freeway was completed through all of Philadelphia by the end of 1985. Running along the western side of the Delaware River for 19.2 miles in the city, this was one of the most expensive roads built up to that time. Costs rose to $17 million per mile in the riverfront quarter.

The Crosstown Expressway would have connected to I-95 at South Street. Thankfully terminated in 1974, this project would have taken out a block-wide swath of the city between the Delaware and Schuylkill Rivers and would have decisively separated South Philadelphia from Center City. The Vine Street Expressway does essentially the same thing river to river between Vine and Callowhill, dividing North Philadelphia from the city's core.

Federal regulations enacted in 1966 mandated an archaeological investigation prior to construction of any project involving federal funds. Archaeologists were thus able to examine some of the I-95 corridor during the freeway's formation. They dug into the project site as wrecking balls knocked down forsaken warehouses and row houses around them. As darkness fell, collectors looking for bottles and pottery would scour the great gorge. Artifacts not pillaged were pulverized by bulldozers or reburied under tons of concrete.

One wonders what could have been found had there been a proper archaeological exploration. There certainly would have been more traces of wharves and docks. But what other treasures could have been recovered? Perhaps a Quaker spy's gate pass, an old tavern sign, a drunken Indian's pipe, some pirate booty, a sail maker's toolkit, a Swede's prayer book, an Italian immigrant's passport…

Epilogue

This was the story of the Delaware River in central Philadelphia, with an emphasis on the public stairs that William Penn directed to be built and the streets along the Delaware's edge.

Needless to say, the eight-hundred-pound gorilla in the room is Interstate 95. The highway creates an immense physical barrier that separates walkers, bikers and even motorists—not to mention entire communities—from the river throughout Philadelphia. The I-95 divide is psychological in places, so urban planners hope that landscaping and other improvements will help alleviate the problem and get people to cross the highway to the Delaware. But there's no disguising or denying that I-95 brutally severs the waterfront of Philadelphia from the rest of the city, especially Center City, and it makes Penn's Landing underwhelming as a space for recreation.

Yet this is merely the outcome of a much larger, more poignant issue. Simply put: the worst part of an Interstate being built through Southwark, Society Hill and Old City Philadelphia in the 1960s and '70s is that the physical record of almost three hundred years of Philadelphia history was thoughtlessly obliterated. The memory of countless Philadelphians living, working, eating, drinking, shopping, visiting and even dying on the Delaware's west bank during this time has been lost and forgotten.

It should also be noted, as a final wistful comment, that the superhighway covers the spot where William Penn, the great lawgiver, humanist and real estate developer, first set foot on Philadelphia soil.

Epilogue

And for what purpose? Just to allow anonymous motorists from parts unknown to pass through Philadelphia in the blink of an eye?

This utter lack of respect for Philadelphia's past would be unthinkable if the artery were constructed today. Other options would definitely be explored besides routing a noisy fifteen-lane expressway through such an important (yet admittedly shabby) part of Penn's City. Even the possible submersion or demolition of the highway, proposed as of late, could never restore what is gone forever.

Ultimately, though, this has been an account of how the city of Philadelphia has related to its principal river over time. The story is one of ongoing conflict between various uses of the Delaware and the city's original waterfront, ranging from commercial to transportational to residential to recreational. It began playing out in the late seventeenth century during the time of William Penn and Samuel Carpenter. Later, Stephen Girard and Paul Beck contributed greatly to how the story played out. These and other noteworthy men and women molded the riverbank over time and were intimately involved in what happened along this two-mile-long strip of land.

In conclusion, the continuing saga of the Delaware River's western embankment is more relevant in the twenty-first century than ever as the City of Brotherly Love finally rediscovers and reclaims its historic waterfront.

Further Reading

Two fairly long documents referenced in the text are available on the Internet. One is the "Regulation of the Bank of the River Delaware," executed by William Penn's agents on April 26, 1690. This act appears in *A Digest of the Ordinances of the Corporation of the City of Philadelphia, and of the Acts of Assembly Relating Thereto* (1834 and 1841 editions). The other document is the statute authorizing the City of Philadelphia to fulfill Stephen Girard's will: "An Act to Enable the Mayor, Aldermen and Citizens of Philadelphia to Carry into Effect Certain Improvements, and Execute Certain Trusts" (P.L. 176, March 24, 1832). Girard's will is also available online.

Brandt, Francis Burke. *The Majestic Delaware: The Nation's Foremost Historic River*. Philadelphia: Brandt & Gummere, 1929.
Carpenter, Edward, and Louis Carpenter. *Central Riverfront District Plan*. Philadelphia: Philadelphia City Planning Commission, 1982.
———. *Samuel Carpenter and His Descendants*. Philadelphia: Lippincott, 1912.
Corcoran, Irma. *Thomas Holme, 1624–1695: Surveyor General of Pennsylvania*. Philadelphia: American Philosophical Society, 1992.
Cotter, John L., Daniel Roberts and Michael Parrington. *The Buried Past: An Archaeological History of Philadelphia*. Philadelphia: University of Pennsylvania Press, 1993.

FURTHER READING

Foster, Genevieve. *The World of William Penn.* Philadelphia: University of Pennsylvania Press, 1973.

Franklin, Benjamin. *The Autobiography of Benjamin Franklin.* New York: Books, Inc., 1932.

George, Alice L. *Old City Philadelphia: Cradle of American Democracy.* Charleston: Arcadia Publishing, 2003.

Hogarth, Paul. *I.M. Pei and Society Hill: A 40th Anniversary Celebration.* Collingdale: Diane Publishing, 2003.

———. *Paul Hogarth's Walking Tours of Old Philadelphia: Through Independence Square, Society Hill, Southwark, and Washington Square.* Barre: Barre Publishers, 1976.

Ingram, Henry Atlee. *The Life and Character of Stephen Girard of the City of Philadelphia, in the Commonwealth of Pennsylvania, Mariner and Merchant.* 6th ed. Philadelphia, 1886.

Jackson, Joseph. *Market Street, Philadelphia: The Most Historic Highway in America; Its Merchants and Its Story.* Philadelphia: Public Ledger Company, 1918.

Keyser, Charles S. *Penn's Treaty with the Indians.* Philadelphia: David McKay, 1882.

La Roche, R. *Yellow Fever, Considered in Its Historical, Pathological, Etiological, and Therapeutical Relations.* Philadelphia: Blanchard and Lea, 1855.

Mease, James. *A Memoir of William Penn.* Philadelphia: Association of Friends for the Diffusion of Religious and Useful Knowledge, 1858.

———. *The Picture of Philadelphia, Giving an Account of Its Origin, Increase and Improvements in Arts, Science, Manufactures, Commerce and Revenue.* Philadelphia: B. & T. Kite, 1811.

Modjeski, Ralph, et al. *The Bridge Over the Delaware River Connecting Philadelphia, P.A. and Camden, N.J.: Final Report of the Board of the Engineers.* Philadelphia: Delaware River Bridge Joint Commission, 1927.

Murphy, Jim. *An American Plague: The True and Terrifying Story of the Yellow Fever Epidemic of 1793.* New York: Clarion Books, 2003.

———. *On the Delaware River: The Port of Philadelphia.* Philadelphia: Department of Wharves, Docks & Ferries, 1921.

———. *Penn's Landing: A Master Plan for Philadelphia's Downtown Waterfront.* Philadelphia, 1963.

Pennypacker, Samuel Whitaker. *Philadelphia and Its Environs: A Guide to the City and Surroundings.* Philadelphia: Lippincott, 1893.

———. *Philadelphia Rapid Transit: Being an Account of the Construction and Equipment of the Market Street Subway-Elevated.* Philadelphia: Philadelphia Rapid Transit Company, 1908.

FURTHER READING

———. *The Port of Philadelphia*. Philadelphia: Department of Wharves, Docks & Ferries, 1930.

———. *The Port of Philadelphia: Second in the United States: Its History, Facilities and Advantages*. Philadelphia: Department of Wharves, Docks & Ferries, 1926.

———. *The Settlement of Germantown, Pennsylvania and the Beginning of German Emigration to North America*. Philadelphia, 1899.

Powell, John Harvey. *Bring Out Your Dead: The Great Plague of Yellow Fever in Philadelphia in 1793*. Philadelphia: University of Pennsylvania Press, 1949.

———. *The Proposal for a Covered Below-Grade Expressway Through Philadelphia's Historic Riverfront*. Philadelphia: Philadelphia Architect's Committee, 1965.

Ritter, Abraham. *Philadelphia and Her Merchants: As Constituted Fifty and Seventy Years Ago*. Philadelphia, 1860.

Skaler, Robert Morris. *Society Hill and Old City*. Charleston: Arcadia Publishing, 2005.

Smith, Philip Chadwick Foster. *Philadelphia on the River*. Philadelphia: Philadelphia Maritime Museum, 1986.

Taylor, Frank H., and Wilfred H. Schoff. *The Port and City of Philadelphia*. Philadelphia: 12th International Congress of Navigation, 1912.

Trussell, John B.B. *William Penn: Architect of a Nation*. Harrisburg: Pennsylvania Historical and Museum Commission, 1980.

Watson, John F. *Annals of Philadelphia and Pennsylvania, in the Olden Time; Being a Collection of Memoirs, Anecdotes, and Incidents*. New York: John Penington & Uriah Hunt, 1844.

Weld, Isaac. *Travels Through the States of North America…During the Years 1795, 1796 and 1797*. 2nd ed. London, 1799.

Wildes, Harry Emerson. *The Delaware, The Rivers of America*. New York: Farrar & Rinehart, 1940.

———. *Lonely Midas: The Story of Stephen Girard*. New York: Farrar & Rinehart, 1943.

Winch, Julie. *A Gentleman of Color: The Life of James Forten*. New York: Oxford University Press, 2002.

———. *Workshop of World: A Selective Guide to the Industrial Archeology of Philadelphia*. Wallingford: Oliver Evans Press, 1990.

Yamin, Rebecca. *Digging in the City of Brotherly Love: Stories from Philadelphia Archaeology*. New Haven: Yale University Press, 2008.

Index

A

Alfred (Black Prince) 95
American China Manufactory (Bonnin and Morris Works) 120
American Clyde. *See* shipbuilding on the Delaware
American flag mural. *See* Philadelphia Warehousing and Cold Storage
archaeology by the water 31, 111, 162
Arch Street 59, 60
  Arch Street Wharf 60, 61, 62, 131
Association Battery 121

B

bank houses 38, 43
bank lots 16, 17, 38, 127
Bank Meeting House 59
bank steps 7, 14, 18, 28, 29, 50, 56, 60, 63, 67, 69, 85, 86, 98, 132, 148, 156

Beck, Paul, Jr. 136
Belt Line Railroad. *See* Philadelphia Belt Line Railroad
Benjamin Franklin 33, 76, 79, 86, 89, 100, 110, 121
Benjamin Franklin Bridge 33, 49, 50, 69, 83
Blackbeard (Edward Teach). *See* pirates on the Delaware
Black Horse Alley and Steps 85
Blue Anchor
  Landing 101
  Tavern 101, 103, 105
Blue Cross RiverRink 147
Bonnin and Morris Works (American China Manufactory) 120
Bookbinder's Restaurant 93
buried treasure. *See* pirates on the Delaware

Index

C

Callowhill Street 25, 27, 28
Callowhill, town of 27
Camden, NJ 32, 33, 48, 82, 83, 105, 137, 139, 148, 154
Campington (British Barracks at) 19
Carpenter, Samuel 16, 88, 89, 92, 128
  Carpenter's Stairs 89
  Carpenter's Wharf 88, 89, 143, 161
Cavanaugh's River Deck 21, 24, 27, 37
caves on the riverfront 14, 38, 40, 43, 99, 155
Charter of Privileges for inhabitants of Pennsylvania 32, 91
Cherry Street Steps 56, 58
Chestnut Street 81, 88, 147
  Pier (5 South) 87
Christ Church 79, 80
City Tavern 75, 90
Clifford's Wharf 63
Coast Guard Station Philadelphia 126, 152
Cohoquinoque Creek. *See* Pegg's Run/Willow Street
Columbus Boulevard. *See* Delaware Avenue
Columbus Monument, The 142
Comfort Inn Downtown 78
Consolidation of Philadelphia (1854) 25, 48
contagion and vermin along the wharves 53, 60, 130
Coocanocon Creek. *See* Dock Creek
Court at Old Swedes 115
Crooked Billet Steps/Tavern/Wharf 86
Crosstown Expressway 114, 162

D

Dave & Busters 37
Delaware Avenue 15, 20, 69, 78, 95, 100, 133, 134, 137, 139, 140, 141, 142, 144, 155, 157
  Elevated 69, 87, 158
  Market 106
  nightclubs on 21
Delaware Expressway 15, 27, 31, 59, 107, 147, 148, 157, 163
Delaware Indians. *See* Lenni-Lenape Native Americans
Delaware River 7, 9, 11, 13, 62, 84, 99, 137, 139, 141, 155, 163
  Trail 126
  Waterfront Corporation 52, 84, 126
Delaware River Bridge. *See* Benjamin Franklin Bridge
Delaware Skyway 157
Dock Creek 95, 99, 101, 106, 110
Dockside Condominium. *See* Residences at Dockside
Dock Street 97, 100, 101, 105

E

East Central Incinerator 20
Elfreth's Alley 58, 59
Evans, Oliver 62

F

ferries crossing the Delaware 32, 33, 69, 82, 83, 84, 137, 138, 154
Ferry Branch or Ferry Line. *See* Delaware Avenue Elevated
Festival Pier 20, 147
Filbert Street Steps 69
fishing on the Delaware 13, 76, 84, 109
Fitch, John 61
Floating Church of the Redeemer 104
Foglietta Plaza 106, 107, 161

INDEX

food distribution on the waterfront 27, 76, 98, 100, 111, 112
Forten, James, Sr. 113
Frankford Elevated 69
Frank Winne & Son 66
Front Street 16, 17, 23, 43, 44, 45, 46, 56, 59, 60, 66, 68, 71, 92, 96, 99, 102, 106, 127, 160

G

gambling along the river 41, 141, 155
Gazela 150
Girard Group Piers. *See* Piers 3 and 5 North (New Girard Group Piers)
Girard, Stephen 63, 65, 67, 71, 79, 97, 130, 132, 133, 137, 142, 164
Gloria Dei Church 117
Goodisville 141, 142
Great Conflagration of 1850 47
Great (Quaker) Meeting House 78

H

Head House Square 99, 111, 112
Hertz Lot and West Shipyard 30, 31
High Pressure Fire Service building 54, 56
High Street. *See* Market Street
High Street Market 76
High Street Wharf. *See* Market Street Wharf
Holme, Thomas 56, 60
Hopkins, Samuel 62
hostels by the Delaware 68, 78, 86, 89, 90, 92, 101, 111, 138, 139
Humphreys, Joshua (and Humphreys' Shipyard) 34, 122, 143
Hyatt Regency at Penn's Landing 78

I

ice-skating on the river 35, 147
immigration via the Philadelphia waterfront 37, 125, 142, 148
Independence Seaport Museum 149
India Wharf 92
insurance for commerce 96
Interstate 95 (I-95). *See* Delaware Expressway
Interstate Highway System 157, 160
Irish Memorial, the 148, 149

J

Jersey Market 76
Jupiter (tugboat) 151

K

Key, John 40
Kidd, William "Captain." *See* pirates on the Delaware
King's Highway. *See* Front Street
King Street. *See* Water Street

L

Lenni-Lenape Native Americans 13, 77, 84, 107, 115, 142
Letitia Court (Letitia Penn) 85
London Coffee House 74, 91

M

made-earth 14, 30, 78, 117, 134, 137, 146, 155, 158
Man Full of Trouble Tavern 102
Market Street 74, 76, 77, 78
  Subway 69, 158
  Wharf 82
Market Street Wharf 76, 82
Merchants' Exchange 97

171

INDEX

military activity near the riverside 19, 44, 89, 95, 116, 121, 123, 124
millionaires on the waterfront 64, 66, 92, 93, 113, 137
Mischianza 118, 147, 151
Moshulu 37, 151

N

New Jersey ferryboat disaster 154
New Market. *See* Head House Square
New Sweden 23, 115
Noble Street 22, 25, 26
North End 23, 25, 109
Northern Liberties District 19, 22, 23, 25, 27, 29, 39, 48, 59, 107

O

Octo Waterfront Grille 21, 37, 49
Old City Philadelphia 81, 85, 144
Old Swedes' Church. *See* Gloria Dei Church

P

parks along the Delaware 20, 87, 91, 107, 126, 138, 144, 147
partying by the Delaware 20, 37, 118, 152
Pastorius, Francis Daniel 40, 113
Pegg's Run/Willow Street 22, 23, 25, 45, 104
Penn's Landing 11, 15, 87, 144, 145, 147, 157
  Trolley 140
Penn's Landing: A Master Plan for Philadelphia's Downtown Waterfront 145
Penn's Landing Corporation. *See* Delaware River Waterfront Corporation
Penn's View Hotel/Ristorante Panorama 68
Penn Treaty Park/Monument 77, 107
Penn, William 7, 9, 13, 17, 23, 27, 28, 29, 40, 41, 45, 56, 77, 80, 85, 88, 91, 99, 101, 107, 108, 109, 129, 156, 163
Penny Pot Landing/Vine Street Landing 32
Penny Pot Tavern 31, 40, 102
Philadelphia Belt Line Railroad 139, 140
Philadelphia Customs House 96
Philadelphia Department of Wharves, Docks and Ferries 36, 71, 87, 142, 144
Philadelphia Korean War Memorial 107
Philadelphia Maritime Museum. *See* Independence Seaport Museum
Philadelphia Navy Yard 123, 124, 150
Philadelphia Vietnam Veterans Memorial 107
Philadelphia Warehousing and Cold Storage 20
Piers
  1 and 3 South 87
  3 and 5 North (New Girard Group Piers) 11, 71, 73, 146
  5 South (Chestnut Street Pier) 87
  8 and 9 South 98
  9 North 53
  10, 11 and 14 South 98
  12, 13 and 15 North 49
  16, 18, 20, 22, and 24 South 98
  19 North 36, 37, 125
  24, 25 and 27 North 25, 27
  30 South (Kenilworth Street Pier) 154

INDEX

34 South collapse 126, 152
36 South 116
38 and 40 South (Southwark Group Piers) 118
53 South 125
Piers at Penn's Landing (Condominiums). *See* Piers 3 and 5 North (New Girard Group Piers)
pirates on the Delaware 103, 137
  Blackbeard (Edward Teach) 103
  Kidd, William \ 104
places of worship by the river 59, 78, 79, 104, 117
pollution of the waterways 23, 84, 99
Port of History Museum. *See* Independence Seaport Museum
Port of Philadelphia 10, 67, 96, 142, 143, 149
Port Wardens (Board of) 36, 137
Proposal for a Covered Below-Grade Expressway Through Philadelphia's Historic Riverfront, The 158, 160
Proprietary/Propriety of Pennsylvania 15, 16, 17, 127, 128

Q

Queen Village. *See* Southwark District

R

Race Street 51, 52
  Connector 51
  Pier (10/11 North) 53, 55, 126
railroading by the water 24, 25, 27, 49, 69, 82, 98, 124, 140
Rat Receiving Station 53

Regulation of the Bank of the River Delaware 128, 129
Residences at Dockside 154
restaurants along the waterfront 21, 37, 68, 93
Ride the Ducks 62, 152
Ridgway House Hotel 78
Ridgway, Jacob 78, 138
Ridgway Park 138
Ristorante Panorama/Penn's View Hotel 68
riverboat gambling 155
RiverLink Ferry 84, 138
Rock Lobster. *See* Octo Waterfront Grille
Rush, William 46, 122, 123

S

Schuylkill River 9, 44, 62
Shackamaxon 107
Shambles. *See* Head House Square
Sheraton Society Hill Hotel 111
shipbuilding on the Delaware 14, 30, 34, 122, 123, 150
shipping to and from Philadelphia 9, 25, 26, 34, 37, 49, 64, 71, 72, 93, 118, 137, 142
Skid Row of Philadelphia 27, 141
Skylink Aerial Tram 148
Slate Roof House 91, 99
Smith's and Windmill Islands 137, 138, 139
Society Hill Philadelphia 110, 112
Society Hill Towers 78, 111
Society of Free Traders 109, 111
Soupy Island 139
South End 109, 111, 114
South Street 69, 114, 162
Southwark District 111, 114, 115, 117, 118, 122, 124, 125
Southwark Group Piers (38 and 40 South) 118

173

INDEX

Sparks Shot Tower 116
Spring Garden Street 19
SugarHouse Casino 21, 155
Summer Street Steps 50
Swanson Street 115, 116
Syng, Philip, Jr. 86

T

tall structures by the waterside 45, 64, 78, 79, 97, 111, 116, 123, 154, 155
Tamanend, Chief 77, 107
taverns along the waterfront 31, 41, 74, 86, 89, 90, 92, 101, 102, 114, 141
Treaty of Amity and Friendship 77, 107
Trotter, Nathan (Nathan Trotter & Company) 66
Tun Tavern 89, 95

U

United States
  Marine Corps 89, 95
  Navy 95, 122, 124
  Patent No. 1 62
USS (United States Ship)
  Becuna 107, 150
  Mississippi 123
  Olympia 150
  Pennsylvania 123
  Randolph 122
  United States 122

V

Vine Street 14, 32, 46, 59
  Expressway 43, 162
  Ferry 33
  Landing/Penny Pot Landing 32, 33, 35
  Pier (19 North) 36, 37, 125

W

Walnut Street 95
Wharf 93, 96, 138, 154
Washington Avenue 120
  Green 126
  Immigration Station 125, 126, 149
Waterfront Square Condominium 37, 154
Water Street 14, 30, 31, 50, 102, 104, 116, 127, 129, 130, 132
Welcome Park 91
West Shipyard and Hertz Lot 30, 31
William Cramp & Sons Shipyard 34, 35
Willow and Noble Streets Group. *See* Piers 24, 25 and 27 North
Willow Street and Willow Street Railroad. *See* Pegg's Run/Willow Street
Windmill and Smith's Islands 137, 138, 139
Wood Street 14, 28, 30
Wood Street Steps 7, 14, 18, 28, 30
working on the waterfront 25, 26, 30, 34, 49, 58, 98, 99, 113, 120, 125, 142, 155

Y

yellow fever epidemic of 1793 60, 130

About the Author

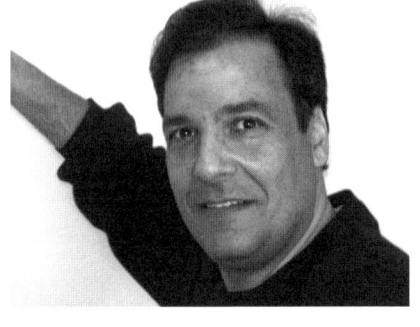

Harry Kyriakodis is a staff attorney for the American Law Institute and ALI-ABA Continuing Professional Education. He is a producer of teleseminars for ALI-ABA and has been the librarian for both organizations since 1992. A historian and writer about Philadelphia, Harry has collected what is likely the largest private collection of books about the City of Brotherly Love: about two thousand titles, new and old. He is a founding/certified member of the Association of Philadelphia Tour Guides and has lived at Pier 3 Condominium at Penn's Landing since 1997, when and where his fascination with Philadelphia's waterfront district began. Harry regularly gives walking tours and presentations on this and other unique yet unappreciated parts of the city for various groups. He is a graduate of La Salle University (1986) and Temple University School of Law (1993) and was once an officer in the U.S. Army Field Artillery.

Visit us at
www.historypress.net